1850 431

D1587751

TO LIVE LIKE EVERYONE

ALSO BY

ANATOLY MARCHENKO

From Tarusa to Chuna

My Testimony

ANATOLY MARCHENKO

TO LIVE LIKE EVERYONE

Translated from the Russian by Paul Goldberg

I.B. TAURIS & Co Ltd
Publishers
London

Published in 1989 by
I.B.Tauris & Co Ltd
110 Gloucester Avenue
London NW1 8JA

British Library Cataloguing in Publication Data

Marchenko, Anatoly
    To live like everyone
    1. Soviet Union. Dissidents. Marchenko, Anatoly
    I. Title
    364.1'31

ISBN 1-85043-159-0

Printed and bound in Great Britain by
Biddles Ltd, Guildford and King's Lynn

FOREWORD
BY ANDREI SAKHAROV

THE WORDS that have become this book's title were repeated to the author throughout his life. "Live like everyone," some said with concern, others with narrow-minded contempt, still others with hatred.

People like Marchenko—people of immaculate honesty who are prepared to make any sacrifice in the name of moral principles—share a tragic yet happy fate. As I leaf through the pages of his life, I always picture his wife, Lara, beside him, and though prison separated them, they seemed always together.

What is this book about? Chronologically, it is about the period between what is described in the remarkable *My Testimony* and the events of the 1970s and 1980s that are only partially recounted in *From Tarusa to Chuna*. Yet this is also his summary (albeit not a completely finished or "polished" book), which contains more judgments and reflections than either of the other two.

The book describes the first few months of a former (and future) convict's freedom. The descriptions are filled with pain and suffering, giving us a glance at the world inhabited by millions of people who live "where the asphalt ends."

The second part of Marchenko's new book tells about the writing of *My Testimony*, about the creative pains of the author and his struggle with the covert—and sometimes quite overt—enemies of his book. *My Testimony*

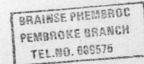

was the first book about post-Stalin camps and prisons, the first extensive testimony about this shameful underside of our society. The book played an important role in the formation of the human rights movement in the USSR and around the world. The authorities could not forgive Marchenko for his heroism. So he was tried and sentenced. Twenty years of suffering, then death in Chistopol Prison were part of his extended sentence.

The third part of the book is a record of the cat–and–mouse games with the KGB, a trial, then once again, the camps. Here we get the inside picture of the camps, with a multitude of details that supplement *My Testimony*. The book ends with the legal farce of a personal trial on Article 190-1, for slander of the Soviet system, one of the first trials on that article. The book reflects the many tragicomic—but in their essence purely tragic—characteristics of the subsequent ritual observances of this type.

By opening Anatoly Marchenko's final book, the reader will sense the fate and the soul of one of the most remarkable people of our time.

Andrei Sakharov
January 23, 1987

INTRODUCTION

To Live Like Everyone would have been the name of my novel, but its drafts were confiscated in so many KGB searches that I have set it aside for the time being. Yet when I sat down to write this memoir, I realized that I am the one the title speaks to, that all my life I have been told to live like everyone else. So I lifted the name of my own would-be novel.

To Live Like Everyone, like my other two books, *My Testimony* and *From Tarusa to Chuna*, is nonfiction. Chronologically, it fits between them.

Those familiar with my books will easily detect that this one is different.

First, it is heavier on discourse, on attempts to fathom the past, present, future; to visualize my own tomorrow, the tomorrow of my country, and that of the world. *To Live Like Everyone*, though it is based on specific events in my life, is more subjective than my other two books.

Second, there are almost no names here. This is deliberate, and here is the reason: I don't want to bring harm upon good people. Believing in the maxim that "every country must know its stoolies," I am always prepared to name those. But what's to be done about honest, decent people who—risking no less than I—helped me? And not me alone.

It is all the more inconceivable to name those who did a lot of good, useful work, but did it quietly, announcing nothing, attempting to conceal it from the authorities. Lawful actions of today could be the criminal offenses of tomorrow.

I don't always hazard naming even those who, after having done a lot of good here, were forced to emigrate. It would seem they are out of danger, so I could express my gratitude and admiration. But, considering the peculiarities of the path of our historic development and our "national traditions," I cannot allow myself even that. In this country no one—and nothing—is forgotten. It could happen that some of the émigrés would want to return to the Motherland—or come to visit relatives. The authorities would then have grounds for blackmailing them.

For the same reason I cannot mention several facts and anecdotes that would otherwise merit inclusion— events so specific that the authorities would have no problem determining the names of those involved. Perhaps a KGB agent or another official, in a one-on-one encounter, expresses sympathy or even offers to help. What is he, a provocateur or a genuine sympathizer? I don't know. Still, I have no right to imperil him by describing such an episode in detail. It's a pity that such things must remain untold.

My intention is to make the reader see beyond the altered initials, beyond the anonymity of heroes, beyond the cipher of anecdotes. I want him to visualize, to sense, the people who shaped my writing and my relatively untroubled (in the Russian sense of the word!) fate.

They are the people thanks to whom it is still possible to live and breathe in our country.

TO LIVE LIKE
EVERYONE

1

I HAD DONE six full years in camps and prisons for politicals.

At the time, nobody—anywhere—under any circumstances said as much as a word about the existence of political prisoners in the USSR.

The world was alarmed by the conditions of political prisoners in South Africa, Portugal, Franco's Spain, and South Vietnam, but not in the USSR. We simply did not exist. And this injustice made us climb the walls.

Ours was the despair of men condemned to oblivion.

I, too, was appalled by the world's shameful silence. But I was just as appalled by our own conduct: it was up to us, the prisoners, to speak out—and to speak out loudly.

How many political convicts I had seen go free! There were Ukrainian, Lithuanian, and Latvian nationalists who so loudly cursed the USSR, "the prison of nations"; there were those imprisoned "for the war," and those convicted in the post-Stalin era. There were thinking men among them, even writing men. Each of them, while he was behind barbed wire, raged and fumed along with everyone else, accusing the whole world of being Khrushchev's, and later Brezhnev's, accomplice. But after getting out, they'd become free men again, so they didn't think twice about the suffering, about those who stayed

behind. Could this be explained by a simple human shortcoming—cowardice?

I had no doubt—and have none to this day—that many decent and intelligent people were among those who went free. But even now, as I am writing this, the old question comes back: Why? Why hadn't any of them brought our suffering to light?

Just about every man can say honestly, "I am not a writer." Besides, it's not enough to write. One must also be able to publish.

There were people I could talk to, share ideas and plans with. How many times have we discussed this question! There, behind barbed wire, in the shadow of guard towers, all of us saw only one way to let the world know: break out of the USSR, find a journalist, and tell him all there is to tell.

It would be better to do this without leaving the country; "a voice from within" would have more credibility, we thought. But none of us had any doubt that if anyone attempted such a thing at home, his fate would be sealed immediately and irreversibly: he would rot in prison or be knocked off quietly. I felt so much anger for myself and for others that I was prepared to risk even that, but felt that without help I would be unable to handle the writing end of it and sending my work to the West.

We read all the newspaper stories about Sinyavsky and Daniel, and I paid particular attention to the fact that they had sent their manuscripts to the West. All I could do was envy their ability to write and the connections it must have taken to dispatch manuscripts abroad. My own "connections" didn't give me a faint hope of finding even a tiny crack into the free world. Only the first option, crossing the border, seemed feasible, so I decided to attempt it.

In the camps, *zeki*, the convicts, have been known to make escape plans: from tunneling to ballooning to staging an armed uprising and breaking out to freedom. The more daring try to carry out such plans, paying no mind to the risks involved. For the most part, such attempts end tragically. But some succeed, and those who do become the stuff of legends. I'd heard rumors about someone who, back in the Stalin era, managed to break out of the camps, then crossed the border. There, the story went, he had published a book.

"Crossing the border? It's worth the risk," I thought then.

On the day I was released from the camps, I couldn't get up the nerve to tell my friends that our plans were not to remain worthless prison banter. Ashamed of using bold words, I didn't even hint at my final determination to act on our dreams to expose the Soviet system of political camps to the world.

I HAD no intention of finding a place to settle down for good. I figured I was taking a short vacation to prepare for crossing the border. I wanted to lie low for a while; get a residence permit, a job, a place to live; look around. Besides, I wanted to go back home, to see the folks. It could have been the last time.

When I went to Moscow it was for a day or two. I had a few messages from other zeki to their relatives. But that visit to the capital stretched out and became decisive in shaping my subsequent life.

From day one, my new Moscow acquaintances treated me with attention and care. To them, I was a man "from

3

out there." Their warmth was genuine, and I felt a little awkward to be receiving their respect for no particular reason, not through any merits of my own, but simply because I had just been released from a camp for political prisoners and because I came highly recommended by other inmates.

In our country, and especially in Moscow, a prison record isn't a novelty. It's hard to find a family of the Moscow intelligentsia that hasn't been touched by the Stalin terror. Thanks to Khrushchev, a wave of rehabilitated "enemies of the people" swept through the city. The unprecedented humanitarian gesture of allowing former convicts to settle in the capital had for a long time created the illusion that political trials and political prisoners had become a thing of the past.

In Moscow, I was asked many questions about the conditions in the political labor camps, and I saw that this wasn't idle curiosity. These people were indeed ready to help. My new acquaintance A, for instance, immediately started to correspond with my friend V, who had served eight years and had seven more to go. She sent him books (at that time book parcels were still allowed), wrote about Moscow theaters and exhibits, sent New Year's presents to his children, visited his mother. A and V remained friends even after V's release.

If anyone had kept track of correspondence to the camps, the numbers would have shown a leap in 1966. Books, letters, and reproductions of paintings were arriving in a steady stream. They weren't sent by the prisoners' relatives but by complete strangers.

This made me realize that prisoners like me had felt isolated simply because there was no information about us, not because nobody cared.

Those were active times. In the camps, I didn't think

our intelligentsia was capable of such bustle. Here, in Moscow, I saw that even a conversation over a cup of coffee wasn't wasted.

I shared my plans with a few of my Moscow friends, not holding back that I would like to cross the border and seek help from a Western journalist because I would not be able to write the book myself.

I must say that my new friends were skeptical about this plan. They said that trying to cross the border would be suicidal. "Write it yourself. Write it as you tell it," they said. "Let's see what comes out."

I hadn't renounced the plan I made in the camps. I'd simply altered it.

A SHORT TIME in Moscow cured me of all prejudices about the intelligentsia. Those prejudices, I think, were typical of anyone who grew up deep in the provinces.

I grew up among children of railroad workers. Our parents weren't called engineers or brakemen; all railroad workers went under the same name, *mazutniki*, greasers. Black industrial fuel literally dripped off their clothes. They stewed in it.

Our two-story wooden barrack had twenty-four rooms inhabited by twenty-four families. There was a kitchen for every three families. Thank God there were only four of us. Some of our neighbors had seven or eight people to a 16-square-meter room.

There were times when Father returned from a trip and we had a visitor, say a neighbor or a relative from the village. He'd have to wash up right there, in the room, by the stove. And when he needed to change, Mother took a blanket off the bed and, standing in front of him, blocked him from the visitor's view. That scene was so commonplace that our neighbors didn't think it necessary to walk out of the room, even for a minute. It wasn't unusual; that's the way all of us lived. But when a woman mazutnik changed clothes, the men among the guests generally walked out.

All of us heard the same admonition from our parents: "Study! Study if you don't want to end up like your father, a mazutnik for life!" To their children, parents presented their profession as a curse. To live means to suffer; to work means to work like a mule. That was the philosophy of my parents' existence.

Our parents' favorite role models were people of "clean" professions: teachers, doctors, the manager of the train depot, the director of the bread-baking plant, the secretary of the regional committee of the party, the prosecutor. All of them were regarded as part of the "intelligentsia." True, teachers and doctors didn't live any better—some lived worse—than us, but we regarded their work as clean and easy. The others I have listed, in the eyes of everyone in town, were at the peak of comfort and prosperity.

After I reached adulthood, I retained the old, settled image of the intelligentsia as people who don't work like mules, or, to put it simply, people who are paid for doing nothing, just for being there.

You can imagine our opinion of people whose names began with "Dr." or "Prof." Possession of such a hypnotizing prefix, we thought, was equivalent to possession of a magic wand. Life within that stratum, we thought, was a year-round Shrovetide (there were no such people in our town), and those people's work, besides being easy and pleasant, guaranteed each of them a luxurious apartment, an automobile, and other possessions our parents couldn't even dream about.

Writers and members of the Academy of Sciences seemed like the gods to us. Of course, our thinking about them was twofold. On the one hand, everyone knew that they busied themselves with work that was useless to the point of absurdity. A pen pusher lies like a dog barks! A scientist breeds some damned flies. We joked about them, even mocked them. Still, we bowed to their omniscience and omnipotence, except, of course, in matters pertaining to everyday life. Every one of us knew that no writer understood "our life" and that no Academy member could cure even a simple boil, whereas Aunt Motya could.

In all, we equated the people of intellectual professions with authority, the "bosses." And what's there to love the bosses for? They are the haves who want to pay the have-nots as little as they can and charge them as much as they can. The teacher, the doctor, the engineer, and—even more so—the judge, the prosecutor, and the writer are all in their employ. Besides, the bosses and the intelligentsia (as well as their children) hobnob with each other, not with simple mazutniki.

THERE WAS no shortage of educated people among political prisoners, but my ties with them weren't close enough to change my preconceptions. Still, after some reflection, I began to distinguish between true intellectuals and people of clean (nonmazutnik) professions. The former had my respect. They seemed to have a sense of decency and morality, a quality one begins to truly appreciate amid the cruelty of camp life. I became friends with a young man named Valery Rumyantsev, formerly a KGB officer. Despite his cursed former life, I think he was a true intellectual. There is a lot of him in me to this day. Toward the end of my term, I became friends with the writer Daniel and the engineers Ronkin and Smolkin. To my surprise, I didn't sense in them the alienation I had felt on the outside, so I concluded that the alienation was partly the product of my imagination and partly that of circumstance and prejudice.

Still, it's one thing to become friends with someone in the camps; it's something else to preserve that friendship on the outside.

In the camps we are all equal. Our garb's the same; the rations and the punishment cells are the same; the bunks we polish with our emaciated bodies are the same; the guard detachment is the same, too. We take part in the same conversations, and our interests are the same. "It seems they wound up in the camps because they aren't like everyone, because they are white crows," I thought.

My prejudices were strong when I first found myself among the Moscow intelligentsia. But in my dealings with them, I felt no insincerity on their part. At first, I kept a watchful eye on those people. I was afraid of missing anything that would confirm my prejudices.

Finding myself in the company of these better educated and more refined people didn't make me lose self-confidence. It wasn't insecurity on my part; it was exploration.

I didn't go out of my way to get acclimated. I'd say I behaved naturally, not trying to impress anyone. But, for all I know, others could have seen it differently.

Ten years have passed since my first encounter with the Moscow intelligentsia. Looking back, I see how lucky I have been in life, how much I have learned from these people.

They shattered my belief that the authorities have destroyed just about all that was vibrant in this country, and that in the camps they are trying to finish off what little had survived. I thought the so-called Soviet people were an obedient flock, with every member deprived of an identity. And then, in Moscow, I met an entire social stratum that denied the Soviet "successes" in bringing up "the New Socialist Man, the Man of the Future."

My circle of acquaintances grew daily, but it was still measured in dozens of people. "You call that a social stratum," a skeptic might say. "It's a pocket of resistance, if that. Sooner or later, there will be places for all of them in the camps." That's true. In the last ten years many of these people have gone through camps, prisons, internal exile. Many more have emigrated to the West. Still, to this day I am convinced that they were more than a small group, more than a few outstanding individuals. They were a social stratum of opposition to the official hypocrisy, mandatory ideology, and the regime as a whole. I think this stratum is composed of the finest part of our intelligentsia. The number of people is small, but, unfailingly, new ones come along to take the places of those who have been jailed and those who emigrate. Hypocrisy and lies contradict human nature, and that is why this stratum has formidable inner strength.

Now I know that this stratum isn't just a Moscow phenomenon. It can also be found in some of the bigger provincial cities. Of course, life is harder for dissenters in the provinces: everyone knows what everyone else is doing; the repressions are more ruthless. This makes dissident circles smaller and not as open as in the capital. Still, they exist, and that's the most significant achievement of the post-Stalin era. The regime softened up a little, and right away, people became more decent. They began to trust each other, even if that newfound trust was limited to close friends. Of course, there's always a risk of encountering indecency, cowardice—even a KGB agent or a provocateur—but I am not talking about the exceptions; I am talking about an unexpected and joyous phenomenon.

I KEPT meeting new people, and sometimes, large groups showed up at the apartment where I was staying. Even before my arrival, that apartment had turned into the nerve center of political activity. Friends and acquaintances came to ask Larisa Bogoraz about her imprisoned husband, Yuli Daniel, and his codefendant, Andrei Sinyavsky. Often they came by simply to chat and exchange news. Conversations continued till dawn; no subject was barred, no discussion "forbidden." There were people to argue with, people to agree with. In that group it was no great sin to be alone in a point of view.

In late 1966, I got to see the tail end of the letter campaign in defense of Sinyavsky and Daniel. You can imagine the effect these petitions had on a man fresh out of a camp for politicals. People were openly defending the right to free expression and uncensored art, taking the side of the two men who'd had the courage to publish their work abroad! These petitions were signed with real names; even the professions were listed! Holy shit! I'd seen people sent to the camps for less.

I read a few samizdat works, including *The White Book*, a compilation of documents about the Sinyavsky and Daniel trial. I also met the author of *The White Book*, Aleksandr Ginzburg. Until then, I had read no contemporary literature, save for propaganda and works approved by the Glavlit censors. These other books were my introduction to freedom and independent thought. It was so unexpected, so new.

I met a few of the authors. They weren't aspiring leaders. They weren't heroes. They were ordinary people: a history teacher, a mathematics teacher, an artist, an editor, a few writers and scientists. Many of their names began with those hypnotizing prefixes, "Dr." and "Prof." I grew ashamed of my old prejudices toward them. The intelligentsia had a lot more to lose than we, the workers, and, of course, a whole lot more than convicts. A zek has nothing to lose. He lives by the Bulat Okudzhava song

> *Forgetting all the cares, all former cares*
> *There is no job and there's no pay . . .*

So a zek fights his battles, not giving a damn. But on the outside, a man risks his career, his family's well-being, and not just for a short time, but, as the saying goes, "to the end of the power of the Soviets." And that's not to mention the possibility of arrest.

On top of it all, I learned that the intelligentsia wasn't living the good life I had envisioned. The first family to invite me to their home were Natalia Sadomskaya and Boris Shragin. They were husband and wife, both social scientists. They lived in a 15-square-meter room in a "communal" apartment, the kind shared by a number of unrelated families. Both had to work at home, but when one was at the typewriter, the other had no place to work. Their neighbors always milled around in the kitchen, one of them always hissing. Boris, who had a doctorate, made a little more than a laborer, about 170 rubles a month; Natasha made much less since she was yet to defend her dissertation. I don't recall ever seeing Boris in a decent suit, even after she, too, had earned a doctorate. As for Natasha, I always picture her in an old overcoat, which I bet she inherited from her mother.

That's how most of the intelligentsia lives. To make ends meet, many give lessons, translate, do reviews; I know a few people who spend vacations working with construction crews in Siberia.

Their living conditions, I would say, are no better than those of workers. A worker, at least, has a chance to get an apartment through his plant. But a teacher, a doctor, or a scientist waits ten years or so to get an apartment through the Moscow city bureaucracy. Many don't even qualify to get on a waiting list.

Reading samizdat, I learned how destitute some of the writers were during the Stalin era. Even after Stalin, it is up to the authorities to decide which of the writers are to be well fed while others get scraps or nothing at all.

Curiously, my childhood preconceptions about "government servants," such as KGB officials, prosecutors, and militia employees, survive to this day. My Moscow friends had few kind words to say about those people, and, of course, vice versa. Some examples:

"Ha! You call him a writer. He doesn't own more than one pair of pants," Investigator Pakhomov of the KGB once said of Sinyavsky while interrogating a witness in the case that put the writer behind bars.

"You call them intelligentsia! All they got's one suit in the closet!" Investigator Gnevkovskaya of the Moscow prosecutor's office said after conducting a search of an apartment.

On another occasion, First Lieutenant Kuzikova of the Tarusa Militia Department found a man without residence papers staying at the house of one of the "subversives." Filling out a report, she learned that the man was a research fellow at a Moscow institute.

"How much do they pay you?" she asked.

"One hundred and fifteen rubles a month."

"And you call yourself a research fellow?" said Kuzikova, a scornful smile on her face. "Even *I* get a hundred and seventy rubles."

There you have it: the skills our country values most.

2

A YEAR AND A HALF earlier, in the camps, I miraculously survived a bout with meningitis. I had gotten no medical care, so during my first week on the outside I wanted to see a doctor.

A doctor at a for-fee clinic wrote his diagnosis: I needed to be hospitalized for surgery on my left ear. He couldn't direct me to a hospital, though. For that I needed to go to one of the "regional," free clinics. To get an appointment at a free clinic I needed a Moscow residency permit, which I didn't have. I went to the Ministry of Health, where I was given a written authorization to see a consulting physician at the Botkin Hospital.

There, once again, I was told that I needed to be hospitalized for ear surgery "at the place of residence." That meant the hospital didn't want to treat me.

Had I collapsed in a Moscow street, an ambulance would have taken me to a hospital where I would have been admitted with or without a residence permit. But I didn't want to wait that long, and feigning a disease was something I had never done—even in the camps.

My Moscow friends came to the rescue. Using their connections, they placed me in a hospital under the care of a friend, a surgeon. He wasn't just any doctor; I was left in good hands.

Friends visited me daily. They brought books or delicacies, or simply stopped by to entertain me. After getting the impression that I had a passion for Marxist literature, Ludmilla Alexeyeva brought over a volume of Plekhanov. There may be people who think the differences between Plekhanov and Lenin are significant, but after reading a few articles, I decided that Plekhanov was well qualified to give Lenin lessons in spinelessness.

In the hospital I got to read *The Master and Margarita*, Mikhail Bulgakov's just-published novel, which had all of Moscow talking. That was my first encounter with that magnificent Russian writer.

Everything about *The Master and Margarita* was startling: the novel itself, its publication after a thirty-year ban, the very fact that it was serialized in *Moskva*, an otherwise useless magazine which now became impossible to find. (At the time, I could not have even suspected that within a year I would deal with that magazine head-on.)

Bulgakov's line "Manuscripts don't burn" is more than words of inspiration. It's a warning to the hangmen of literature.

After checking out of the hospital, I read another Bulgakov work, *The Heart of a Dog*. How much longer can this book be kept under lock and key! Will it ever be published in the writer's Motherland? Later still, I read his letter to Stalin. It showed just how courageous and decent a man Bulgakov was.

I checked out on January 20, three days before my birthday. But since January 23 fell on a Monday that year, we decided to celebrate a day earlier. I was surprised— pleasantly—that the party was more than a quiet gathering of friends. It was a big celebration. It seemed my birthday was a good excuse for old friends to gather around the table, meet new people, and exchange bits of news from around Moscow.

It was unlikely that anyone at the table could have predicted that Aleksandr Ginzburg, one of the guests, had just one more day of freedom.

For now, at the party, he was accepting compliments for *The White Book*, which everyone at the table had either read or heard about. KGB agents tailed Ginzburg wherever he went, and he sensed that his arrest was near. Meanwhile, Ginzburg's demeanor was calm, natural; he drank moderately, was moderately upbeat. But twenty-four hours of freedom was all he had left.

WHILE I was in the hospital, friends found me a place to live in a village near Maloyaroslavets. I went there the day after the birthday party. I returned that night, my residency permit application stamped with resolutions of the regional militia precinct and the oblast department of the Ministry of Internal Affairs. There were no written explanations, just the word "Refused." In conversations with the militia, I usually got a better explanation: "We've got enough of your kind as it is."

To this day, I am convinced that suffering only begins after release from the camps.

How many oblasts I had wandered! How many cities, towns, workers' settlements! And how many villages I had passed through, trying to get a place to live! At one jurisdiction the militia declined my application because the place I'd found was near the Leningrad-Moscow Highway. Another time I was told that the comprehensive plan of the town's development stipulated that the side of the street where I found a room to share was slated for demolition and redevelopment within thirty-three years, by the year 2000. Or, they said, the room I had found was one square meter short of meeting the "sanitary code." Typically, the officials laughed in my face while saying this.

All these travels got on my nerves and eroded my small savings. What's worse, time was slipping by fruitlessly. And I had little time to spare. Spending three days in the same place without an internal residency permit is a violation of passport rules. Three such violations, and it's back on trial and back to the camps. That's the vicious circle: the law says, get a residency permit, but the militia refuses to issue it, knowingly and deliberately making you a "criminal." Not every ex-zek gets out of that one.

That's not all. Released convicts are automatically vulnerable to another criminal charge: if you don't work for four months, you are a "parasite," and that, too, carries legal penalties. (Who cares if you've done six years in the camps and saved up enough money to survive for six months.) And surely nobody cares that there's no way to get a job without first getting a residency permit!

My four months were running out. After that, if they decided to get me, or if they just happened to snatch me up, there'd be nothing to stop them from carting me off. I had to do something; I had to act fast.

The only solution that came to mind was to continue my feverish search for a place to rent and a permit to live there. I won't describe all my travels. That would make fatiguing, tedious reading. It was the same thing everywhere. But I will describe one trip to Kursk.

A friend of mine had a friend or some other connection there, so he decided to take time off and go with me. So there we were, in Kursk. That year, 1967, spring came early, and the end of February was warm and muddy. There was no frost, except at night. My friend's connection worked in the medical institute, so we had no problem finding her. To our disappointment, she said that she was pessimistic about our undertaking and that she didn't know how she could help. She said Kursk was overcrowded, and finding a place there was next to hopeless. Since her job included finding lodgings for students, we believed her.

"There's not enough dormitory space," she said. "So we get them residency permits for the dorm, but they live elsewhere, renting cots in private homes."

Be that as it may, we didn't want to leave without trying our luck. We spent the whole day running around the city, finding nothing. On the walls, utility poles, and bulletin boards we saw plenty of ads: "Looking for a room or bed," "Husband and wife looking for a room or bed," and so on. But there wasn't an ad offering that room or that bed.

We tried knocking on doors on the outskirts, but that, too, led nowhere. I must say that I am not spoiled when it comes to living quarters. Still, housing problems in Siberia of 1957 weren't as bad as in central Russia of 1967, the fiftieth year of the Soviet state.

Private homes were filled with renters, some of them single, some with families. But for the most part, landlords preferred single women and were reluctant to rent to men. Typically they rented out space for a bed, and the beds were often shared by two strangers. In one of the houses I was offered a bed to share with another man—for ten rubles a month. I would have taken it, but the deal didn't include getting me a residency permit. Others in that house were students, and all of them (with the exception of my would-be bedmate) were registered residents of the university dorm or the laborers' dorm. So the deal fell through.

There was no shortage of "laborers wanted" notices pasted around town. When we went to those places and asked if residence would be provided, we found that some places had no space in laborers' dorms and others simply had no dorms.

My friend, unlike me, was a shrewd man with a gift for making contacts. At one plant, he struck up a conversation with a manager who had some vacancies to fill. They seemed to hit it off to the point that my friend gave him his Moscow address and he promised to visit next time he came to town.

"Our dorm's full and the militia categorically refuses to issue residency permits to any of our men," our new acquaintance told us. "So we take on new people without permits, and after they've worked for a while, we get behind them and get them permits."

He also gave us an address and said we must go immediately and check about a cot.

"These people used to rent to a young guy, also from Moscow," he said. "He stayed there for six months, earned a good recommendation from this plant, then went back to his family. Just left a few days ago. Go there, and when you get his place, come back and we'll tell you when you start."

We ran to that address. On the way, I couldn't stop agonizing over the place. Was it still vacant? Or had someone snapped it up? The house, it turned out, was near the plant, just a ten-minute walk. The street, Khutorsky Proyezd, cut through a gully; a steep trail led to the house. Fortunately, the landlord and his wife agreed to rent to me.

They took us to a dark corner, the back of the masonry kitchen stove on one side, a homemade cloth-and-wooden room divider on the other. A small, dark window let in hardly any light, leaving the room in damp semi-darkness. Two iron beds stood across from each other, headboards facing the window. One of them had been made; a small suitcase was tucked under it. The other stood bare, its ancient steel mesh ripped and thickly covered with rust. The space between the beds was about a meter. A wire stretched from the door to the window ran through its center. Hanging on it was a color-speckled rag, a room divider.

"Two student girls sleep on that one," the woman said, pointing at the made bed. "The other one's vacant. It's yours if you're satisfied with it."

I would have been satisfied with any hole. I was tired of looking, was sicker than hell of it. I yearned for a place the way a zek, crammed into a prison train where there's no place to stand up, stretch, or lie down, yearns for the next stop, yearns for a bare bunk in even the worst of cells. That dream, too, doesn't always come true.

"How much will this cost?" I asked.

"I charge the girls ten rubles each," she said. "For you, since it's a separate bed, it's fifteen. Well, sometimes you'll chop some wood, carry in some water."

I was promised a straw mattress and something to use in place of a pillow until I got bedding of my own. I shelled out the fifteen rubles in advance. I was afraid I'd lose the place.

I returned to the plant. In personnel, with no questions asked, they signed my application letter and hired me to load raw bricks into the ovens.

Once again, I was promised that after I worked awhile, the plant would get me a residency permit in the dorm. For now, I would be given a job, but no entry would be made in my passport. So, at least for awhile, I would have all the rights of a bird. I was so happy—things were starting to fall into place at last—that I regarded the unusual terms of my hiring as temporary bureaucratic difficulties which would soon go away.

I was introduced to my brigade leader, and we agreed that the following morning I would receive gloves and a work jacket. I would report to work during the second shift.

In the frenzy of our search, I hadn't paid much attention to Kursk. So that evening, after taking my friend to the station, I decided to walk back and look around.

I didn't like the town. The streets weren't paved, and only the central streets were lighted. Going to the outskirts meant wandering in complete darkness, getting stuck in the slush, and stumbling over potholes.

IT FELT GOOD to walk to work again. It was not that I expected the job to be pleasant. It was just that, having begun to work, I would feel more secure.

Not even a trace of that happiness remained by day's end. It was replaced by disappointment, distress, a sense of hopelessness. It wasn't just that the work was pure servitude; I'd expected that. Something else distressed me.

Other workers told me that all the men in the brigade were just like me, recently released convicts. They were all Muscovites, and they came here to be closer to their families in Moscow. They told me that there was no way to get residency papers in fewer than six months of work.

Many of those people lived right there, at the plant, on top of the brick ovens. At first I didn't believe it, thinking it was just a practical joke they were playing on the new guy in the brigade. But during a smoking break I climbed on top of the oven and, sure enough, discovered the "living quarters." Work jackets, labor-camp pea

21

coats, and other rags were spread out on top of the insulation. Each of the residents picked a place. (At least there was no shortage of space here.) A small group sat under a bare light bulb, playing cards. They were filthy, their faces unwashed. They looked like street urchins. Empty food cans, food scraps, and vodka and wine bottles were everywhere. Two workers, in their clothes, slept atop some rags in opposite corners.

Some humanlike being, stooped over and as dirty as the others, was pacing in semidarkness, fiddling with oven shutters. Nobody seemed to notice me. The stooped one, after finishing whatever he was doing with the shutters, passed by me on the way to the ladder.

"New, huh? Fresh from the camps?" he asked without much interest.

"Yes."

"When did you get out?"

"Four months ago."

"Picking a place?"

"No, I'm renting one."

"Oh."

He went down the ladder, and after standing around awhile, I followed him.

There was something odd about that plant. Being inside and blocking out such signs of the modern era as trucks and electrical wires, one could imagine himself having been transported miraculously from a modern production facility to a different era, to a plant of the time of Peter the Great.

In those days I was yet to be spoiled by easy labor. I'd done my share of hard and hazardous work in gold and uranium mines. In the Karaganda camps I worked in a rock quarry, where rocks were chipped off with a crowbar, wedge, and sledgehammer and stacked by hand.

At the Kursk plant, workers pushed cars heavily laden with raw bricks toward the ovens. The rails, like the plant itself, were ancient, certainly predating the Revolution. Three or four workers, some of them women (equality!), leaned with their backs against a car, dug their heels into railroad ties, and pushed. Sometimes, on a curve or a bad joint, the car derailed or simply stopped. Then everyone else in the brigade dropped his work and ran to help with the car.

My job was to take raw bricks off the cars and hand them to another laborer, positioned by the oven door. That worker, in turn, passed the bricks to a third, who lay them down for burning. Those two other workers were women.

To fill the day's quota, we had to handle 12,000 raw bricks in eight hours. For that we were paid two rubles, eighty-five kopeks each.

It's not easy to make it on less than three rubles a day. Twice a day I went to the diner near the market. Though the prices there were moderate, I had to shell out eighty kopeks or so each time. That was for cabbage soup "with beef broth base," some cutlet or goulash, and a glass of sour cream. I didn't treat myself to any extras. Twice a day, that's a ruble, sixty kopeks. That left a ruble, twenty-five kopeks for my other expenses. It didn't help that you had to eat on days off, when there was no pay. So you worked just so you'd have enough strength for another day of servitude. In the end, there was no money to spare. And then there was the fifteen rubles for my bed; that was five days' wages to be carved out of the food budget.

My job was easier than some. I'd seen men pull bricks out of the ovens. Now that was true servitude! To meet the plant's quota, the bricks were pulled out of the oven before they cooled off, to make room for more. The men worked with their shirts off. They loaded bricks into massive wheelbarrows and wheeled them outside. Their pants were always soaked with sweat. I don't know how they managed to avoid colds. After all, there were still frosts at night.

During their dinner break, the workers rarely went anywhere. They ate at the plant, sitting on broken bricks, in the dust. There was no shortage of jokes, nearly all of them indecent. Every joke got a laugh. Most of the brigade was young, and the young always want to laugh, no matter how tired they are, no matter where they are. Many of them, just like me, didn't have residency papers, but they went on with their lives, they kept on hoping.

The thought of residency papers never left me. If I were to write about the camps, I needed my friends' advice and help. Besides, I felt that it would be hard for me to lose touch with the social activism I had encountered in Moscow. But going there without the appropriate stamp on my passport was risky. What if I were stopped by the militia? How would I prove that I was not a drifter? It didn't seem likely that my brick plant would do much to rip me out of the claws of the Ministry of Internal Affairs. And at that time, I simply didn't want to get a jail term for no reason. So I figured I'd work a whole week, walk into the personnel office, and ask some hard questions. The manager who hired me wasn't there. I tried again, but he wasn't showing up. (Later I found that I wasn't the only person he'd "helped," and those others had reserved their choice curses for him.)

My life was monotonous outside work, too. Usually after coming home, I dropped off to sleep. I hadn't had a job for four months after the camps, and I'd spent some of that time in the hospital. Now, at work, I tired easily.

I'd been out of the habit once before, during my pre-trial investigation. But in the camps I got back into it, working like everyone else.

In the camps we usually gave the new guy a couple of days to catch up, helping him a bit so he wouldn't just plunge into work, letting him get into it gradually. But here, on the outside, the new guy was expected to work with the others, not slowing down the pace.

Sometimes I surprised even myself by how tired I got. After throwing 12,000 bricks, I couldn't feel my hands. The rest of my body didn't feel like my own either. Others in the brigade knew how I felt—they'd been there themselves—so they poked fun at me. Their humor was always the same: would I, in my physical condition, be interested in dragging some Valyukha into a corner? Valyukha herself, usually right there, also had a choice word or two.

To this day I can't fathom what drives our Valyukhas to such servitude. They were, after all, Kursk residents, so if they wanted cleaner work, it was there for them.

I was spending nearly all my free time searching for a better place to live. I felt like a king by comparison with those who lived atop the ovens. I'd gladly have shelled out half my pay, cutting into my meals at the diner, just to have a place of my own.

My relationship with the girls and the landlord was the best one could imagine: we hardly saw each other. I did hear the two girls; I sensed them. And sometimes, under the curtain, I could see two or four girlish feet. As for the four other girls who shared the adjoining room, I saw them only once, on Sunday, and not all of them. The landlord treated me well. I guess it was convenient to have an invisible renter.

After a week, I stopped over at personnel, to remind

them about myself, to say that it would be nice of them to get me a residency permit.

"Work for five or six months, then we'll help with a residency permit," the woman said.

"So I have to spend six months with all the rights of a bird?"

"Hey, what if we helped you with residency? You'd run away the next day. We've seen a lot of migrants like you."

"But that will last until the first encounter with the militia." I tried to convince her.

"So don't get caught by the militia," she said.

I left with nothing. The mood I was in, I could have just hanged myself. Six months! That was easy to say. There was no way I'd chase seventy-five rubles a month doing this servitude. When I was looking for a room, I'd figured I'd get residency papers, quit that job, and get another.

The following day I turned in the work jacket, took my pay, and caught a train to Moscow. My mood was rotten. There I was, once again returning to Moscow with my suitcase, light as a ballerina's, a towel, soap, and a change of underwear inside it. I was ashamed to return with nothing accomplished, as if this failure, like others before it, was a fault of my own.

In Moscow, I got a few more addresses to check out, but once again, the militia refused to issue residency permits. So I decided to go to my parents in Siberia. Surely I'd get a permit in Barabinsk. And if I got turned down the first time, my relatives would help, they'd find a way. I'd get a job, too. Meanwhile, my Moscow friends would be able to find me a place closer to them. And when I returned from Siberia, my passport would have a residency permit stamped on it, plus a stamp indicating that

I'd been employed. That would relegate the camp to the past. I wouldn't be a zek trying to find a place to grab onto, but an upstanding citizen moving from one residence to another. It could be that the militia would then get off my case.

On the day of my departure from Moscow, Natasha Sadomskaya invited me to hear her defend her dissertation. I hadn't had an occasion to witness a dissertation defense before, so I was curious.

Natasha is an ethnologist, and her dissertation was about the Basques, their ethnic characteristics and national self-awareness. I couldn't understand the scholarly aspect of the problem, but the talk about the Basques' national consciousness made me recall some Soviet analogies: there are many nationalists in the camps, whose interest in similar problems had led not to a professorial podium but to the "defendants' bench" and a place behind barbed wire.

I can't remember what sort of arguments followed Natasha's presentation. I do remember noticing a young man named García. (Later I found out he was one of the "Spanish children" who were brought to the USSR in 1938, after Franco won the Spanish Civil War.) I remember he was talking about some peculiarly Basque method of fishing. Natasha, a Spanish specialist, could learn such details only from books; she hadn't a prayer of visiting the site of her studies. On the whole, García praised the dissertation.

I felt out of place at the Ethnology Institute. Everyone I passed in the hall was a scholar of some sort. I was an outsider. But when I sat down and looked around, I noticed a few familiar faces and, after a while, began to feel more at home.

A large sheet started circulating in the room. On it,

everyone was asked to put down his name and the institution he represented. These were places like Moscow University, Science Publishing House, history research institutes. When the sheet reached me, I signed it. But which institution did I represent? What should I put down? The gulag?

A mischievous thought flashed in my mind. "Institute of Marxism-Leninism of the CPSU Central Committee," I wrote. After all, in the camps I had read the complete works of Vladimir Ilych, published by that very institute. So, in a way, I really am its alumnus. The camps can be regarded as an institute of Marxism (though they are an arm of the KGB and Ministry of Internal Affairs rather than the CPSU). After completing that "course of study," few alumni remain Marxists.

A banquet was to follow the dissertation defense, but I had a train to catch. I said good-bye to my friends. Natasha, disappointed that I wouldn't be able to celebrate with them, ran out of the room and returned carrying a package. In it was a big piece of cake that was to be served at the banquet.

I ate it on the train.

3

I'M HOME. Barabinsk is a small town between Novosibirsk and Omsk. I haven't been back in ten years.

My parents live fifteen minutes from the station. As I walk, I look around. Nothing has changed, as if ten days, not ten years, have passed.

I don't know how much Barabinsk has changed from 1967 to this day. I don't know if new plants have sprung up or if they've paved another street. But then, in the spring of 1967, all but the two central streets were dirt and dust. On the outskirts, the streets were cleaner. In the summer, they cover up with grass. There is one change: the new bus service. Still, the most prevalent vehicles on the road are trucks, which shroud the passerby in flour-fine dust. There are still hardly any cars, but there are more motorcycles, which whiz by me with a racket.

As in the past, there's a narrow booth of an outhouse in every yard. People are carrying buckets to water pumps.

I turn into a short dead-end street, School Street. There are only eight houses here, four on each side. I can see our house from around the corner. We built it in 1954. I was sixteen then. I helped my parents build it, but got to live there for just one year.

It was my parents' dream to own a house. Everyone in this town dreams of it. We had no money for construc-

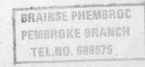

tion, but we did have free labor: my father's, my mother's, and mine. The walls are made of cement with gravel, construction materials that don't cost too much. Railroad workers are allowed to take gravel for free. We needed a lot of water for pouring the walls, so we dug a well, eventually to be shared with our next-door neighbors, the Radchenkos, who had also been our neighbors in the apartment building.

The same well would allow us to water the vegetables in the summer, we hoped. We had to dig deep, 10 meters or so, but the water turned out to be unfit for drinking, partly because we used freshly cut wood to line the well's walls. So in the summer we carried drinking water in buckets from the water pump; in the winter we pulled our buckets on a sled. The closest water pump was half a kilometer away, on Lenin Street in the center of town. As for our well, it produced enough to water the orchards on even the hottest summer days.

We joined forces with the Radchenkos. One day we'd pour our walls; the next day, while ours were drying, we'd pour the Radchenkos'. Our houses are the same: 5 meters by 8 meters, with a room of about 20 square meters and the kitchen about the same size. It took about six weeks to pour both places. After that, there was no shortage of work to be done. We put up the roof, then Father made the floors. My little brother, Borya, and I helped as best we could. We did it all ourselves, all but the stove, which we had to hire someone to build. By the fall we moved into our own house, then waited till the following summer to do the plastering. That gave the place a chance to dry and settle.

By the spring, we started a vegetable garden. Now Mother had still more work to do. We had a cow, a pig, and chickens even when we lived in an apartment. (Our barrack was surrounded by shanties for animals.) And we used to grow potatoes on a private plot outside the town. There was no other way to feed a family. It wasn't just that my father's pay wasn't enough to feed four. There was no place to buy food even if there had been money to buy it with. During my seventeen years in Barabinsk I had never seen butter in a state store, just margarine and "combined fat," and even that wasn't always there. Meanwhile, wagonloads of butter were leaving our train station. I used to load it during school vacations. Rarely did we have butter on the table, and when we did, it was either bought at a farmers' market or brought by relatives from the village. I guess it wasn't traditional to eat butter; we got used to living without it, like everyone else in town.

We lived better than many families, especially those with lots of children.

"My children never went hungry, and they were dressed like princes. Take Tolik, he has a leather jacket and a concertina," Mother used to brag. I had a bicycle, too, and later, an accordion. (To buy it, I had to sell the jacket and the concertina.)

Mother remembers every item she's bought in the past twenty-five years. They can be counted on the fingers of one hand. And how much work those purchases cost my parents! The cow and the pig had to be fed, and that wasn't easy. The fields where we could cut hay were far away and hard to get to. The problem wasn't in how much hay you could cut, but how you'd get it out. Now folks feed bread to their cattle, but at that time there wasn't enough bread to feed the humans. There was the vegetable garden, the wash, the repairs. All her life, Mother dragged water from the well and the street pump: for the wash, the cooking, the bathing, the cattle.

After she got her own house she couldn't stop cleaning it, scrubbing it, whitewashing it, painting it. She became so accustomed to hard work that she can't stop
even now that she's sixty-seven and in bad health. She
doesn't know how to rest, doesn't have that skill. Father's
the same way. As soon as he gets enough sleep after a
railroad trip, he gets to the chores, chopping wood, repairing the shed, fixing this and that. He did some shoe-
making, too, to earn extra money.

Like the rest of our friends and neighbors, he never
even smelled rest homes and sanatoriums. Vacation time
had to be used for cutting hay, picking potatoes, building
someone's house, or digging a well. Even if he'd gotten
a free trip to one of those places (which he didn't in two
decades), he wouldn't have taken it. No time for that.

Once a year a railroad worker can get free tickets for
himself and the family. And how my brother and I en-
joyed those trips! But those trips had to have a reason to
them, they had to pay for themselves. So we brought
back scarves from Orenburg and apples from the south.
Not for ourselves, but for sale. Once, I remember, we
brought apples from my aunt in Central Asia, and I got
to sell them one at a time on the railroad bridge. Still,
we ate a lot of them during the trip.

SPRING HAS COME to Barabinsk. The snow is gone, to-
mato seedlings are seen on every windowsill. I'm sure
Mother's windows, too, are green with seedlings.

Father is probably at work, and Mother at home. I
hadn't told the old folks I'd left Moscow.

Of course, there are the inevitable laments and tears,
how thin I'd become, how unhealthy, how dark-skinned.
But even in her laments, Mother doesn't stand still. She
brings out what food she has, then cooks some more. She

32

is as swift as I always remembered her, except now she seems to have grown older and, somehow, even shorter than she used to be.

As we wait for Father to come home from work, Mother gives me all the news. Father's finishing his last days before retirement. Next Saturday, she'll give a party to which she has invited Father's entire brigade. Therefore, Mother has a lot of work to do: she has to get the alcohol, cook for twenty people or so, clean the house, wash and clean everything.

Father hasn't changed much, just dried up a whole lot. He has more gray in his hair than in 1946, when he came back from the army after surviving the entire siege of Leningrad. A few years ago he was moved from the engineer's helper's job to that of a carpenter. That's because electric engines had come to the Barabinsk depot, so the workers with some education were retrained to use them, while the illiterate and the barely literate, like my father (he can sign his name and barely reads newspaper headlines), were transferred to whatever jobs came along. Of course, a carpenter's life is easier than a railroad worker's, but the pay is cut in half, and that determines the pension.

In the corner I spot the old 40-liter can that I remember from our house construction days. Mother used it to boil homemade brew for the "construction helpers." And even after construction, the can rarely stood empty.

In my childhood, Mother frequently beat me with a rope from the well bucket. Sometimes it was for a good reason, sometimes for no reason at all. My offenses included raiding the neighbors' orchards, pranks at school, mixing with the "wrong crowd." But my parents were never in the habit of hiding anything in the house, not the money, not the food, not the homemade brew.

So, at about age fourteen, to my friends' envy, I had free access to the brew can. There were times when I drank a whole glass, but I never got drunk.

Later I began to drink more, though not because I got away from my parents' control. It's just that I had more reasons to drink, more "co-bottler" friends. I was fortunate to begin my working career at a Komsomol construction project, in the mines and among the miners, in other words, just where the drinking is heaviest. I don't know what my relationship with the bottle would have come to if it weren't for one incident that made me swear off the drink. It happened in the winter of 1957. I worked as a driller in a mine near Tomsk. It was a tradition in our little settlement to spend days off drinking. One Sunday, after drinking all day and getting amply soused, I decided to go to a dance.

It was 40° below Centigrade outside, but I walked out wearing just my shirt and light shoes. Nobody in the house was in any shape to stop me, or to tell me at least to put on some warm clothes. Had I been sober, I would have made it even in shirtsleeves. It wasn't my first frost, after all. But after climbing over a fence, I fell in the snow and couldn't get up. I would have frozen to death had not other young people, also going to the dance, pulled me out and dragged me to the club. There I sobered up a bit, and, toward the end, did some dancing and walked some girl home, first stopping at my place to get a coat and a hat.

The following day, at work, I realized what had happened. Though I drank a lot, until then I had never drunk myself into the horizontal position. I used to be proud of that talent of mine. After that night, I became scared. I wasn't so much afraid of freezing to death; I was more afraid of becoming a cripple. What if I had frozen off my arms and legs? Under the steady banging and gnashing of my antediluvian KA-2M-300 jackhammer, I thought of my uncle Misha Mikheyev, who had no arms. They were amputated after he got drunk, fell in the snow, and froze. When I was a child, he scared me with his black stumps. I started to picture myself without arms, my imagination searching for examples of helplessness. You can't even button your fly! To be only nineteen and to have black stumps! No, I'd sooner take a rope around my neck. And that's what killed my interest in drinking.

I hadn't had a drink in ten years. On my first day in Moscow I surprised my new friends by refusing the traditional shot glass. Almost all of them drank, some seriously. But, respectfully, they left me alone.

Now, in Barabinsk, I faced the prospect of three parties in a row, one for my father's retirement, another for my return, and the third for my younger brother's coming back on leave from the Fleet.

It's traditional to honor the released zek, visiting soldier, or simply any relative with ample drink. Every family, even the poorest, somehow scrapes together the money for such an occasion. Most can't afford to treat a big company to store-bought vodka and wine, so *samogon*, moonshine, and homemade brew come to the rescue. Samogon and homemade brew are everywhere, in every home. Even a lonely old lady has a jar. What if family comes to visit—or why not pour a glass for the driver who's hauled in firewood or the mason who's fixed the stove, or the carpenter, or who knows whom else?

I didn't want to drive my parents to unnecessary expense; besides, I can't stand drunken camaraderie. I managed to convince my old folks to wait for Borya and celebrate both our arrivals at once.

4

FROM DAY ONE my parents began to ask questions. What was I going to do with my life after the camps?

They wanted me to live near them, in Barabinsk. They wanted me to get married, have a few kids, grandchildren for Mother. In a way they were telling me that since I hadn't managed to break away from the crowd, to distinguish myself, it was time for me to learn to live like everyone.

I had something different in mind. But I didn't want to upset the old folks with my plans. They wouldn't have understood, and they'd have enough grief if I succeeded. Besides, I knew every line of folk wisdom they would have used to talk me out of what I had in mind:

"What do you want? More than everyone?"

"You won't get justice anyway."

"You'd get yourself killed, and there'd be no thank-yous."

There was also a saying based on the names of Soviet newspapers: "*Rossiya*'s all sold out, there's no more *Pravda. Trud* for two kopeks is all that's left."*

Those aphorisms were part of my parents. They were in their blood, their flesh, their bones. They were the

---

*Translator's note: Rossiya is Sovetskaya Rossiya (Soviet Russia); pravda means "truth"; trud means "toil."

words of their suffering: their son had rejected folk wisdom, had remained as wayward as ever. His life was now wrecked.

I rested for a couple of days. I visited the few of my school friends who still lived in town, and, of course, I dropped by the two-story house where I grew up—just to see how "everyone" lives.

In 1967, Grigory was the only one of my childhood friends who still lived there. This is just a decade after there were enough boys my age to form two complete soccer teams. That's not counting the older boys and the younger ones. And there were girls. Now Grigory himself is the father of two children.

Though "the facilities" are still outside, folks in the old building seem to have spread out. In my day, there was a family in every room. Now, it's two rooms per family, with the third room taken up by old people—pensioners. Grigory is lucky. The third room in his apartment was allocated to his mother, so one could say his family has a three-room apartment all to itself. The mother gets a pension, he and his wife work, so there is enough money to get by. Grigory is an engineer's helper on an electric locomotive, basically the same job my father had. The same, but not quite. Our parents were up to their ears in grease, but now, an engineer wears white shirts to work. Our fathers used to spend two or three days on a train; you never knew when to expect them home. Now everything works on schedule, so you rarely put in an extra hour. The old folks who, in retirement, managed to wash the *mazut* off their hands (I thought it would be impossible to get it off) looked at electric locomotive engineers with a certain envy. As for the young ones, they found enough causes for dissatisfaction: "What good is our money if there's nothing to buy: no sausage, no meat, nothing in the stores." "You call that work? You don't get Sundays, you don't get holidays like everyone!"

"Like everyone" means getting nice and drunk on holidays. But the train schedule doesn't recognize holidays. While everyone else reaches for the bottle, a train engineer has to go to work. Even when a holiday and a day off coincide, you still can't get drunk; you have to be at work the next day. The railroad is strict about drinking, so to enjoy life "like everyone," one has to wait till vacation or sick leave.

But, just as our parents said years ago, the new railroad workers say, "God save our children from becoming simple workers like us; let them make something of themselves, let them sign papers at a desk or jabber for a living." That, of course, is pure theory. The kids are lazy bastards, just like we were ten years ago, and the parents are ready to send them off anywhere, be it the army before draft age, a military school, a trade school, or simply to work.

Those were the complaints I heard from Grigory and my other friends traveling the same road as our parents, the mazutniki. However, many of my old friends had more serious troubles. Filipp Pavlov was drinking himself to death; Aunt Pasha, his mother, had cancer (she died soon afterward). Vasya Grebenshchikov got into a university but didn't finish. He went nuts and was committed to a "funny farm" in Tomsk. They said he no longer recognized anyone. Nikolai, Vasily's older brother, was doing another term in the camps. Also in the camps were Romka Vodopyanov, Nikolai Katyushin, Petro Pervukhin, Shurka Tsygankov, Vitka Chernov, Zhenka Glinsky, and our "chieftain," Yurka Akimov. Ivan Sorokin, who went in for robbery while I was still around, was "freed" shortly before the end of his term. He died of tuberculosis in the camps.

As a song goes, "Oh, how everyone from our courtyard has flown so-o-o far awa-ay, here and there, for many, many years."

Vadim Pavlov got drunk and drowned, together with his two "co-bottlers." His brother died of cancer. My namesake Tolik Kopeyko was executed for rape and murder. Mikhail Chesnok, once the Barabinsk celebrity, captain of the all-city soccer team, was stabbed to death by a little squirt half his size. There was no motive for the crime—just a stabbing, that's all. The sister of my friend Volodia Glushanin was axed to death by her husband. My old classmate Volodya Nesmeyanov, nicknamed Academician-President, got in with a gang of hoods, though not too close. By a fluke, he became an accessory to a robbery, after which he went home and shot himself. His death was different from the others; at least there was some reason to it.

I haven't been back for ten years, and how many untimely—and for the most part senseless—deaths there have been in the relatively narrow circle of my childhood friends and classmates! When such news hits you all at once, you are horrified; you sense some kind of epidemic.

All those suicides, those senseless, drunken suicides! All those people killed in auto wrecks, motorcycle crashes, or frozen in the snow! There are several such deaths every holiday.

TWELVE YEARS have passed since my return to Barabinsk, and as I write this, I think of other such tragedies, tragedies that the newspapers never write about.

Chuna, the Siberian settlement where I now live, is surrounded by woods, and in those woods small children have been known to disappear. Recently this happened to a three-year-old girl. Her parents went off to get drunk, leaving her by herself for an entire day and night. They didn't give her a thought until the morning. This spawned rumors that the child had been snatched and killed by the religious fanatics, the Baptists, the "saints," some kind of a religious sect. Such rumors are fueled by antireligious propaganda.

And then there was the plane crash. Residents of a geological surveying camp near Chuna were the first to arrive at the crash site. A few people were still alive, among them an infant; he cried loudly. It happened in December, and the temperature was 50 below. Men and women from the geological camp—they were ordinary people, not bandits—looted the dead, then left. The infant soon froze to death; the crying stopped. Only one passenger survived, a soldier with his back broken. He was being treated at the Chuna hospital, so he told the story.

The inventory of crimes I know to have occurred in Chuna over the few years I've lived here is simply hairraising. There were murders: a man shot his grown son with a hunting rifle and the dead man's mother testified for the defense; in another family, a teenage son shot his drunk father; a woman, aided by her mother and brother-in-law, inflicted knife wounds on her husband, then left the man by the neighbors' fence, where he froze to death; a couple killed their two-year-old daughter (she made their lives difficult); a single mother doused her newborn with dimethyl and burned the body (or, possibly, the live child) in a stove; a man from Odessa was killed for money; a soldier from a construction battalion raped and murdered an old woman; another soldier raped a six-year-old girl.

Nobody claims that all Soviet soldiers are rapists and murderers; still, women are afraid to pick red whortle-berries in the taiga alone.

My life is solitary. I don't follow the "oral newspaper," and only part of the local "Chronicle of Events" reaches me—no more than half. But even that's horrifying, considering that all this has taken place in a town of 14,000 over three years. If this chronicle were to be published in the newspapers, the Chunari would be no less scared than average Americans, who, we are told, are afraid to come out of their houses at night.

Some of them might even start wondering, What is it about our neighbors? What's this "new man" brought up by the socialist system? Today my neighbor comes to me to borrow three rubles; the next day he pilfers the dead and leaves a child to freeze to death! Today he's burning up with enthusiasm, "Fulfill the five-year plan ahead of time!" or some such thing; the next day, for no apparent reason, he hangs himself in his hut's anteroom. I am not saying that all of this is the result of five-year plans or the local schools of political enlightenment. But here's what seems obvious: the social system, be it socialist or capitalist, isn't at the root of the problem. (It's too bad that our propaganda incessantly describes the bleeding ulcers of capitalism; I am afraid our own are just as bad.) The problem is elsewhere, in the peculiarities of our era, in the level of development of mankind. We are all on the same level, irrespective of national borders and polit-ical structures. It would be nice if all of us could get together to find a cure for those afflictions.

But it's not to be! No way. It's "us" and "them"; it's "Their Ways," and "The Soviet Way of Life"; it's "The World of Violence" and "This Is How the Soviet People Act." To keep this differentiation, statistics have been classified, everything from incidence of diseases to crime and accident rates. How can there be any analysis when even our specialists don't know any data? They aren't just hiding information from the enemy; they are hiding it from themselves.

As a result, our criminologists know less about the incidence of crime than do criminals themselves. For instance, the inmates can better judge the occupancy rates in camps and prisons. It's not a pleasant method of inquiry, but I have had many an occasion to employ it.

From 1958 to 1975 I have gone through dozens of transit prisons, never noticing empty cells, or, for that matter, empty cots. Prison regulations entitle you to a cot at these stopovers, but, the odds are, it won't be there for you. As you start to make yourself a home in an overcrowded cell, your place is on the cement floor, by the door, or near the latrine pail; someone gets moved, you move inside, a new man takes your old place. Cells are overcrowded by a factor of two, three, or more.

Every month, a prison system prosecutor walks into the overfilled cell. He stops in the doorway, a notepad in his hands. There's no place to step. "Does anyone have complaints, questions?" The majority of zeki, who are used to living like sardines in a barrel, don't even look at him. Only the new ones, on their first encounter with this guardian of justice, complain about the crowding. "Your cell's not too bad," says the prosecutor.

If the new guy starts to "talk rights" ("I have a right to this; I have a right to that"), he gets another stock answer: "Who invited you here? Is it my fault that there're more of you than we can deal with?"

I guess there's more organized crime in the West. But here we have a horrifying profusion of hooliganism, drunken crimes, crimes without a motive. That's despite the ceaseless surveillance over every man, despite the assumption that every man is a potential criminal. That's also despite residency permits, temporary and permanent. Want to visit someone for ten days? Fill out a form. Where are you from? Whom are you visiting? Why and for how long? Break those rules and it's criminal prosecution. Up to a year in the camps. It's up to the militia to decide whether you can stay. If they decide against you, go on, clear the premises. A militia officer can enter any house, confront anyone. Anyone without a permit? It's a search, and if it reveals someone without a permit, say, an upstanding citizen on a visit, a brother or brother-in-law, wife or son, then the host and the guest share the burden of responsibility. My wife has been fined a number of times. The first time was for not filling out residency papers for her three-month-old son. Then, because I, her lawful husband, was found in her apartment. And last year I was fined because, on a visit, she stayed longer than the permit allowed.

So despite these controls, the New Soviet Man manages to create the sort of crime statistics that the officials dare not publish. He does not seem to lack weapons, say, a brick, a fist, an ax. Even a hunting knife's not something everyone can have; you've got to have a permit— or it's the camps for up to three years. That's why folks here say, "If we were allowed to buy pistols and rifles, like in America, there wouldn't be anyone left to drag the corpses off the streets."

5

It was Saturday, and members of Father's brigade started to file into the house. For the most part, they were young people; just two or three were middle-aged. They were carpenters, plasterers, and bricklayers. They were all dressed well, which was all the more remarkable when I compared it with the Barabinsk garb of old. I didn't know any of them.

Everyone called Father "Gramps," just like they did at work, I suppose. They knew Mother well, they seemed at ease, and it was obvious that they weren't strangers here. Looking at them, I wondered, "What will you be like by the end? How many of you will get home on your own feet?" But I was wrong to think this of them. Nobody got especially drunk, and at the end everyone was still able to walk.

After two or three toasts, the guests became noticeably light-headed and started to sing, dance, and make small talk. Along with the new songs, they sang the old ones, familiar to me from childhood. No get-together was complete without them—"On a Sunday, the Old Mother Came to the Prison Gates Again," "I Was Left an Orphan," "The Rambling Man Escaped from Sakhalin," "The Wild Steppes Beyond Baikal," "The Cossack Galloped Through the Valley," "A Slender Mountain Ash Tree," "On the Flat Plain," "Brown Curls, Sway No More," and so on.

All the guests were aware of my recent past. They even knew that I was just out of a camp for politicals. So, with fear, I anticipated their asking and prying. Discussing serious matters with drunks is not among the world's greatest pleasures. Light-headedness makes every man eager to bare his soul to someone "who understands," to brag about his own bravery and high morals, to say, "The fuck with the Dear Party." But the next day, sobered up, that very man rejoins the obedient herd; out of cowardice and deference he will support and endorse any lowly deed. And if they fire him up a little, he'll even take part in it with great enthusiasm and without a trace of his own thought or personal responsibility. That's why they wag their drunken tongues. They feel no responsibility; it's the wine that does the talking, like their leader. I can't abide drunken bravado and confessions.

But the Good Lord spared me such questions that night.

After the singing, it was time to play some music. So three of the guests and I, with great difficulty, figured out how to connect the new radio, Father's retirement present.

"Just like they say in the newspapers," I said. "Giving a toiler a send-off into deserved retirement, the management presented him a commemorative gift."

The two women helping me laughed loudly, and the young guy made a juicy pronouncement: "You wait for something from our management, you'll eat one cock and shit two out."

It turned out the management had nothing to do with the presents. The workers themselves chipped in to buy a watch and a radio with a record player. They knew that there had never been a radio in Father's house, and that

45

during his whole life of labor he had never gotten around to buying a watch. He didn't know much about watches. The first time his new watch stopped, he more or less figured out how to wind it. But in a week or so, when it needed resetting, he came to me and, embarrassed, asked how to do it. I was more embarrassed than he: after all, a watch was something he should have had from his son.

The management acknowledged Father's retirement with a written notice: Appear in the accounting office to find out the exact amount of your pension. That amount was fifty-five rubles a month, fifty as actual pension, and five for the dependent, the wife. That's for forty years of work, including thirty on a steam engine, including the war, from its first day to the last.

When the guests left and we began to clean up, I asked Father if his brigade members were always this decorous at parties.

"Things happen," he said. "There are times it comes to fighting."

Mother was happy that all had been quiet and peaceful. For years to come she would remember that party and, at every opportunity, tell her friends, "There was enough to drink, all right, but no one so much as said one rough word to one another." That's our custom: to reflect on an evening when no one gets his face bashed in.

Incidentally, anything that stops short of a fistfight isn't defined as an altercation.

UNCLE FYODOR, my mother's brother, threw a party for my brother, Borya, and me, the returning young Marchenkos.

The Barabinsk relatives showed up, and two of Fyodor's sons, Vasily and Vovka, came from Tyumen.

46

Vasily was the oldest, Vovka the youngest. Both were students.

Fyodor's middle son, my namesake, lived with his father and worked as a staff instructor at the Barabinsk Regional Komsomol Committee.

There was samogon, there was singing, and after most of the guests went home, Uncle Fedya, his sons, and I sat down and talked till dawn. I don't know if it was because of me, "the political," or in observance of a family tradition, but everyone was needling the middle brother. Anatoly made no secret of his plans to pursue a party career. He had all the makings of a party official: his every word showed him as a demagogue, a cynic, and a careerist who was prepared to carry out any directive of his higher-placed comrades. With us, blood ties aside, he was officious and condescending, like the enlightened with the unenlightened. Without lowering himself to a debate, he casually explained: "A meeting is an organized undertaking. No one will ever allow it to run in an unorganized manner." This interrupted one of Vovka's pronouncements.

"But don't they ask, 'Does anyone want to speak, comrades? Are there any suggestions?' " Vovka protests.

"That's right, and those who need to speak do so and suggest what needs to be suggested."

"So you mean I can't get up and speak?"

"If it becomes necessary, you could, after preparation. Though with your views, I doubt . . ."

"See, here it is, their fucking democracy!" screams Uncle Fyodor, joyfully elbowing me in the side.

Uncle Fedya had joined the party before the war but never held any party posts. He just ran his diesel and spent many years on oil-drilling expeditions. The party never gave him anything, and his worldview was hardly different from that of my father, who never joined, or from that of other workers. He never felt any responsibility for, or for that matter any pride in, the deeds of the party. "The bosses do what they want and you can't fight them," as the saying goes. Subconsciously, he saw himself as separate from "the bosses" embodied in his own son. "Here it is, their fucking democracy!"

Meanwhile, his son condescendingly explains: "Democracy, you see, is not to be confused with anarchy. You think it's easy to conduct a meeting? It's not like dragging sacks on your hump. If there's no preparation, the dimwits like Vovka here would do their own introducing, seconding, and approving, then would regret it themselves. So at first you get together with the activists, the reliable people, and brief them on the task at hand. Discuss it and decide how to present it to the masses. When the masses are prepared, then the meeting . . ."

"And what if I decide to say what I want, then get up and say it! Without your preparation! What will you do? Gag me?" Vovka is getting more agitated.

"Have you tried to?"

The younger brother is taken aback, but continues: "What the fuck would you do?"

"Just try it. Try it once; if your ass isn't dear to you."

"What does the ass have to do with it?"

Uncle Fedya cracks up once again, elbows me in the side, and screams, "I'll tell you what the ass has got to do with it. I'll tell you! They grab fools like you by the ass and drag you to the KGB!"

"We don't need the KGB for his kind. There are other levers. He's a student."

I ask my namesake only one question: "Tell me, have you had a misfire planning a meeting?"

"Not me," he says. "Others have. But in the final analysis, it's not important . . ."

"Grab the troublemakers by the ass and drag them to the KGB!" roars Uncle Fedya.

"You're behind the times, Dad. Why get your hands dirty with their kind? So what if they scream at a meeting? So what? What does he have to say, this Vovka of ours? He's got nothing to say. So he'd get himself thrown out of school, that's all. The Komsomol instructor, of course, will feel repercussions. Could lead to an official reprimand, or worse, the end of his career. You've got to know how to work with people."

Tolya never made it as a party official. Perhaps he wasn't spineless enough; or he couldn't keep his nose to the wind (a failure of "political sense"); or he didn't cultivate the right connections; or his immediate patron wasn't shrewd enough. It's a competitive field. Nowadays, they are just pushing and shoving. In the late thirties, the price of moving up on the ladder was the life of a predecessor. Consider Brezhnev's climb from a party secretary at a technical school to the top of the pyramid. When I read his biography, I wonder about his predecessors. Why aren't their names mentioned?

Just five years later, three people in that group were no longer among the living. Uncle Fedya, after getting drunk, got on a motorcycle and crashed head-on into an oncoming truck. Vasily, his eldest son, died in a car wreck in Tyumen. Uncle Grisha Pervukhin, who was also at the party, drowned in gasoline. He slipped and fell into the open hatch of a railroad cistern.

I HAD no problem getting a residency permit in Barabinsk; all it took was handing my passport and a draft card to the passport clerk and getting it back right away, stamped.

A few days after my arrival, I started to look for work. I was keeping this secret from my parents. They were trying to convince me not to hurry, but I didn't want to live off them. Besides, I had to save up for the trip back to Moscow and a month or two in the new place.

I could expect to find only the most menial work; my preprison skills were now made useless by partial deafness and chronic otitis. But I lucked out: the bread-baking plant was looking for a porter. I was hired immediately.

Of course, lugging sacks of flour is no easy task, but after a week I got accustomed to it and was lugging them no worse than anyone else. There were three men in our brigade, and our task was to get the flour from the grain elevator to the bread-baking plant.

At the elevator, the sacks of flour are stacked up to about double human height or higher. When you are taking a sack from up high, you pull the sack down on yourself, put it on your back, then lug it. When you get to the bottom of the stack, you need two men to pick up each sack and drop it on your back, and you drag it to a truck, which takes the flour to the plant.

At the bread-baking plant, the process is repeated in reverse. The sacks are unloaded and stacked up all the way to the ceiling. So at first we would drop sacks right on the floor, lay them down like a ladder, then lug our sacks up that ladder all the way to the ceiling. In a shift we unloaded about 40 metric tons, more than 10 tons per person. With the unloading and stacking, that added up to over 20 tons a man. We were paid between 160 and 170 rubles a month. That was the best job I could get in Barabinsk.

Life in the provincial town was stifling. I couldn't find anything to do in my free time, of which I had plenty. I was home at 4:30. After resting up for a couple of hours, then puttering around at home for an hour or so, having nothing to do, I went off to the movies, to catch the late show. Every evening, I found myself enraged by the thought that I was wasting precious time. With such a life-style I could soon wind up like the majority of those who had been released before me. I'd get eaten alive by everyday chores, and lose sight of my main goal. So no one in this world would know a thing about the Mordovian camps—except now that would be my fault.

In the evenings, I would sit down with a notebook. I decided to sketch out some details: describe a few scenes, record some names, events, dates, so I wouldn't forget later. It would be a worthless rough draft; still, that was better than nothing. I could pull something out of it later.

I realized that it wasn't working. I was getting bogged down in petty details, trifling with useless particulars; I was unable to sift and select. I was furious at myself for my inadequacy. And there was no one to tap for advice, no one to show my work to. It was then that I grasped just how badly I needed my new friends, how badly I needed Moscow.

I decided not to wait till I "got rich" at the bread plant but to leave as soon as my Moscow friends told me that they had found me a place to live. Meanwhile, once again in secret from my parents, I frequently went to the railroad to unload gravel, coal, cement, limestone. There they paid as soon as the work was done.

AT FIRST, romantic memories of boyhood made me look up old friends, those who hadn't mastered the sciences, hadn't made something of themselves, but remained in Barabinsk. (Those who finished technical schools settled in big Siberian cities.)

Few of my childhood friends managed to keep from becoming drunkards. Friends don't meet without a bottle; all the talk's about drinking, and football, and your own—or someone else's—family life; so-and-so married so-and-so; those two got divorced a while back; those others are back together again—for the fifth time; this one got deserted by her husband, while that one, conversely, threw his wife out "and she had it coming!"; still others aren't getting divorced, though they live like a cat and a dog. And so forth. All those conversations amazed me by their detachment from everything in the world—even from oneself. Complete alienation from everyone. When we were a group of boys and adolescents, we always stood up for each other, always defended "our own"; then, everyone gets married and friends become nothing but people you drink with. Yes, people still chip in to help with a funeral or get a retirement present like my father's; neighbors will still give you shelter if your house burns down. But that's the continuation of a still-surviving tradition rather than an act of genuine compassion for a fellow man.

Their grumbling about our leaders and social order was getting tiresome, too. I was sick of listening to it. It was always the same thing, the same words, the same recommended solution: hang those whores, hang them all; shoot them all; slash them all; do this to "them all," do that to "them all." And then what? There were no suggestions. If you think about it, they wanted something they already had: a master of their country and their selves, the host of everything, the bearer of responsibility for all. My Barabinsk surroundings depressed and aggravated me. I felt like a stranger in my hometown.

CHUNA IS an even smaller town, even more removed from Moscow.

The people here are the same as in Barabinsk; their interests are the same, the conversations, too. Over the years, I have realized that I was unfair to those folks in Barabinsk. They were living their ordinary lives and had the only interests they could be expected to have. It seems our deferential attitude to our own fate and the fates of others, our idle grumbling, perhaps even our drunkenness are the result of centuries of life under conditions of serfdom, which exists in our country to this day.

Can I be contemptuous of my countrymen because they don't know what they want? After all, my own rejection of the Soviet way of life is no more constructive than their aimless dissatisfaction. Being forcibly entombed, physically and intellectually walled off from the world, deprived of information about ourselves and others, we are capable of nothing more than destructive criticism and advancement of ideas that have no connection to reality.

Then, in Barabinsk, I believed that all of us must stop our normal lives and throw ourselves into insurgency, denunciation of the lie, and insistence on the truth. Had I not decided to write about the camps and had I not passed through Moscow, I might have attempted to "open the eyes" of my Barabinsk friends, throwing my "activism" in their faces. And, naturally, I would soon have crossed into the field of vision of the local KGB, which would have dispatched me to another course of "getting smarter" in the slammer.

But, fearing to burn up for nothing before carrying out my mission, I stayed away from seditious conversations and silently took in the table talk of complaints and profanity.

Only one extraneous event in any way affected that table talk: the death of the cosmonaut Komarov. It gave rise to a lot of rumors and chatter. Such tragedies follow mankind up the path of knowledge and progress. Victims like Komarov are treated with reverence, as martyrs and heroes.

In our closed society, with its rampant sabotage mania, disasters and setbacks are treated as state secrets. The resulting legends can take on curious forms. Nobody believed the official story of Komarov's death.

It was said that after the death of Chief Designer Korolyov, the new designer didn't want to resist government pressure and cleared the flight on an untested spaceship; that Komarov had foreseen his death but didn't dare refuse to go; that when problems developed he requested permission to abort the flight, but the matter took too long to go through the highest channels; that the Americans offered to help, but we declined. Once again a rumor resurfaced that Gagarin was not the first cosmonaut, and that there had been space shots before, all of them fatal to the cosmonauts ("Why do you think they announce a shot when the ship's already in orbit?"); that the first cosmonauts, just after the dogs Belka and Strelka, were death-row convicts (this rumor is particularly widespread in the camps); that Valentina Tereshkova wasn't the first woman in space but we won't ever know her predecessor's name because she was killed. In short, there was an abundance of stories, which ranged from the unbelievable to the plausible.

Some of those rumors were spread by the authorities, evidently to neutralize this ungainly folklore.

An acquaintance of mine told me that at a meeting of activists (he was among them) in the militia, they were given this account of the disaster in space: Komarov's death is his own fault since he went off into space without an order or a go-ahead, before the equipment had been adequately checked. There was also talk of help from the Americans: Patriot Komarov did not accept help from the United States, choosing death in space over betraying the Motherland.

I don't know whether this fairy tale was thrown together on the highest level or in the regional office of the militia. It was completely inept: even in the dinky kolkhoz you need permission to get a horse out of a barn, and there they say a spaceship was taken from the cosmodrome for a joyride!

I, too, viewed the official dispatch with suspicion, if only because it was official. But if you won't get the truth anyway, what's there to discuss?

Another event that shook me up was Solzhenitsyn's letter to the Congress of the Union of Writers. I got its text from Moscow, through unofficial mail. It was a joy to learn that among writers there were people who had not been scared or bought, that even in this country there are people who speak truthfully, without looking back, not stopping to wonder about the consequences.

I wanted to know what our intelligentsia thought of that letter. I had no doubt that many of them agreed with Solzhenitsyn, and that the majority supported his demand to abandon the Glavlit censorship. The letter's

courage and genuine concern about spiritual renewal had to stir those who were still silent, those who didn't yet understand. Even the dim-witted and the hopeless had to stop and think awhile.

In 1977, in internal exile in Chuna, I read in *The Oak and the Calf* that sixty members of the Union of Writers publicly expressed support for that letter. That's an impressive proportion of the several thousand Soviet writers.

In Barabinsk there was no one to whom I could show the letter, no one to share my impressions with. I knew that Solzhenitsyn's yearning for creative freedom was not shared in Barabinsk: it had nothing to do with meat and garb. Perhaps out of desire to toot the same horn with me, someone would say, "It's easy for him to bitch; he's a writer. Those get off scot-free, but if it's one of us, he gets grabbed by the horns—and off to the feedlot."

My parents kept repeating: "Don't go anywhere. Stay here, in Barabinsk. There are people living here, too." Mother kept returning to the subject of my marriage. "How long will you stay a bachelor? Till your beard turns white and no old woman says 'yes'?"

I did my best to laugh it off. "I'll get me a big and feisty one, you'll drag each other by the hair and you won't be glad your son's married."

She went on, unwilling to acknowledge the joke: "You'll live by yourselves, and the old man and I will live by ourselves. There's times when two women in one house don't get along; that's no great misfortune."

God forbid a potential bride should come to our house; the old folks would put treats on the table and do everything to make her like our place and stay longer. Mother's hope was that marriage would give me some smarts, get me attached to the home, so that at last I'd live my life "like a person."

She regarded my Moscow connections with jealousy and hostility. There were times when she bared her soul: "My mother's heart is feeling you'll be back in prison with that Moscow of yours."

My parents heard many of my "seditious" speeches, which they considered blasphemous and leading straight to prison. So they kept repeating, "Why can't you live like a normal person? What do you want from the Soviet state?"

"Just that they stop beating me and others over the head."

"So why's no one beating us over the head? We've lived our whole lives and never once feared prison."

"Mother, even Hitler didn't beat everyone over the head. If you lived by his laws and screamed 'Heil Hitler' you were left alone."

"It doesn't matter what government; if you are against it, it will whop you on the head—and on the ass."

"But in America the Communist Party openly says that it's fighting against the power of the capitalists, and no one's going to prison."

"How do you know? You've been there? You've seen it?"

"It's in the newspapers!"

"Newspapers. What a thing to believe. That's all lies."

"I am talking about our newspapers, Soviet newspapers."

"Oh, the heck with you." Mother waves me off in exasperation. "And whom do you take after, such a clever one? No one's ever been in prison; not in your father's family, not in mine. You've been in twice, and you're still a fool. There are others who learn from prison. It would be better if you drank: a drunk will sleep it off, but a fool—never. As the folks say, 'There's an ugly one in every family.' "

"Weren't you the one who told me that Father's father was executed by Kolchak? And that Uncle Afonya went off to fight for the Reds? And he wasn't of age yet?"

"But they didn't go to no prison. And the times were different. We used to wear *lapti,* and you buy new leather shoes every year, and still nothing's to your liking."

My parents' experience began with prerevolutionary Russia, which, thanks to Soviet propaganda, is symbolized by bast shoes, lapti, as in "lapti-shod Russia." (Incidentally, in Siberia even the hired men had boots.) So they think that the Power of the Soviets put real shoes on their feet.

I've had it with my parents' lapti! To them they are the most weighty argument in support of the Soviet system. If they stop to think, they'd know that shoes, motorcycles, television sets, and other fruits of civilization can be found everywhere in the world, that progress came to us at too high a price. We paid for it with millions of lives. If they thought it through, their heels would burn in those store-bought shoes of theirs.

6

THE NEWS that my friends had found me a place near Moscow came after I had saved up a little money.

But before leaving, I wanted to visit some relatives in the village; would we be fated to meet again? I settled up at the bread-baking plant, then asked my cousin if he would take me to the village on his motorcycle.

First, we decided to visit Mother's brother, Uncle Afanasy, in Zdvinsk, a large Siberian village, a regional center, located on the shore of the Kargat River. Had there been a good road, the trip would have taken about an hour and a half. The way it was, we left after lunch and didn't get there till the evening.

Uncle Afanasy's house is right on the riverbank. There are two of them, he and Aunt Dina. Their six children had grown up and left home. Afanasy looks a lot like my mother: short, wiry, the same facial features. I remember him from before the war, when he rode a sled to our place in Barabinsk, then went out to water his horse at the pump. He would put me on the horse and walk beside it, holding me up with one hand and holding the reins with the other.

He returned from the war draped with orders and medals. He had been badly wounded several times. After the war, despite being barely literate, he managed to finish a course for pyrotechnicians and got a job in road construction. He had visited us a lot then. In 1967 he had turned sixty-five, old enough to get a pension, a small one. So he supplemented it by working as a stoker in the collective farm office. The vegetable garden, too, helped them make ends meet.

Uncle Afonya was happy to see us. Of course, he set the table and got out the traditional bottle, which we didn't touch. He told us that he had stopped drinking altogether. "I've drunk up my share ahead of time, and it's against the rules to quaff someone else's." Mother used to tell me that in his youth Afonya was an accomplished drinker and, despite his size, had a great passion for getting into fights. Though he used to get beat up a lot, he didn't seem to quiet down. But over the years, he started going through "dry periods" when he didn't touch a drop.

Anatoly, Afonya's only son (the rest are daughters), seemed to have followed in his father's footsteps—and then some. He drank heavily even before going into the army, drank in the army, too, and later drank even more. That drunk of a daredevil drives like the wind on impassable roads. He's wrecked a few cars, and he's hit a few pedestrians, but somehow he got away with it, all was forgiven.

Anatoly's wife hanged herself. I guess she couldn't stand such a life. Uncle Afonya took in their two small children, a grandson and granddaughter. He is raising them without his son's help. And he continues to work as a stoker, though now, as I write this, he is pushing eighty.

My father's village, where we were going next, was about 20 kilometers from Zdvinsk. The village's official name is Upper Uryum (it's on the shore of the Uryum

River). Locals call it Lokhmotka,* though the Michurin Kolkhoz here is regarded as one of the most prosperous in the region.

Every other person in Lokhmotka is a relative of mine. Ours is the most common name here, so when they refer to a Marchenko, they add a street name or another distinguishing characteristic, such as "those Marchenkos who live near the store," or "Grandma Lyubka's Marchenko."

The language here is a mixture of Russian and Ukrainian, though there are also words that I haven't heard anywhere else. For instance, godparents are referred to as *lyolki*. Lokhmotka is a settlement of displaced persons, who moved here from Eastern Ukraine after 1910. Now they consider themselves Russians, though residents of nearby villages still taunt Lokhmotkaites with the epithet *khokhly*, the Ukrainians.

Father's family moved from the Kharkov *gubernia* to Siberia sometime in 1914 or 1915. They brought their own agricultural tools (Father still remembers their special horse cart on springs) and got a land allotment of about 80 desyatin.† They had horses, they had other animals, and they lived well, as did other settlers. During the civil war, Lokhmotka sided with the Reds; *muzhiki* went off into the woods to fight Kolchak. My grandfather wrought lances for the partisans. He must have been an intense muzhik. He wouldn't leave his blacksmith's shop even when Kolchak's men occupied the village. So they caught him in the act—and shot him.

After losing its breadwinner, the family became poor.

---

*"The place with rags." (Trans.)
†208 acres. (Trans.)

There was no way a widow with children could work the plot. Father was still a child when he first went to work for rich peasants. He was paid well, he told me; whatever he'd make in a summer would feed the family all year. The employers varied. One treated the hired hands as family; he worked with them, and ate with them, too; and when the time came to settle up, he'd add up more, above what had been agreed on. Another was tightfisted: he paid to the kopek, and didn't feed well. During collectivization, everyone in the village felt sorry for the generous one, and no one pitied the tightfisted one. Father said he was asked to sign a resolution against both *kulaki*, but he refused to denounce the generous one. "He is not rich. He's just bragging. I know him, he likes to brag about his strength and his bravery, too." Of course both the generous one and the tightfisted one were dekulaked and exiled. Had Grandfather been alive, his family might have been dekulaked, too, if only because of their famous horse cart on springs.

The way it worked out, Father became one of the village leaders, one of those who "have been naught" and "shall be everything," albeit lacking an opportunity to earn a piece of bread. It's a good thing he managed to run off to the city in time. Mother grew up the same way, as an orphan in a poor family (though in a different displaced-persons village, that of the Russians from the Orlov gubernia). She, too, had been a hired hand from childhood, and after collectivization she, too, went off to the city.

When I was a child, I spent many a summer in Lokhmotka. Near the village, the Uryum River flows so wide that it looks more like a lake. It's shallow, so you walk a ways to get up to your neck; there are no holes, no whirlpools—a great place for children. The bank is sandy in places, and the sand is white and fine, like flour. Sea gulls raise a never-ending rumpus over the river; in the evenings, rooks and crows join in with a rumpus of their own.

When you get away from the village, the banks become overgrown with reeds that once teemed with ducklings. As children we trapped them the ancient way, using horsehair nooses. We'd hang the nooses, like garlands, around the reeds, cutting off the exit from the reeds to the river. The ducklings would stick their necks in the nooses, then, trying to get out, tighten them. Those nooses were monitored by hawks and eagles, so sometimes all we would find were duck feet and feathers.

In our hunting, we were up to our necks in mud and water; we cut ourselves on the reeds, and we envied adult hunters, who had old guns. Of course, we weren't doing this for amusement: to ward off wartime starvation, we hunted ducks to feed our families.

Fish were plentiful. In those days, we didn't even know about fishing rods. The fishermen stretched their nets between stakes. Everyone had his own place. And when it was time to pull in the nets, the children were called to help from the end that was closest to shore.

In the 1950s nets were banned. Officials from the regional center traveled from village to village, confiscating them.

I HAD a grandmother and a lyolka in Lokhmotka.

Lyolka's father, my great-uncle, whom I called Ded Prokop, died when I was in the Mordovian camps. He was close to one hundred.

Ded Prokop was ancient even the first time I saw him. Half of his head was completely bare, and the hair that scarcely covered the other half was white and fuzzy, like poplar pollen. They say in his youth Ded Prokop had dark features and a shock of thick, black hair, like a gypsy's.

He had the shakes in his head and hands, the result of being shell-shocked and wounded in World War I and the civil war. He had been stabbed, shot through, and slashed. His hands shook so badly that he couldn't lift a spoon to his mouth without spilling. So he drank his cabbage *shchi* straight from the bowl.

For as long as I remember him, Ded Prokop was making something for the kolkhoz: rakes, pitchforks, shovels, scythes. That's how I remember him to this day: at his workbench under a thick bird cherry tree, making scythes or teeth for the rakes. I would climb that bird cherry, to get the biggest berries, the ones up high, and through the foliage, I would look at the old man, in his homespun shirt and pants. The light wind stirred his white, loose-fitting clothes and the white fuzz on the back of his head.

Ded Prokop didn't talk much and was getting to be hard of hearing. But he liked practical jokes. He got me the first time we met.

Grandmother Lukerya gave each of us a bowl of shchi. I noticed that his shchi and mine were different colors: mine was light, his was red. So I kept glancing at his red shchi. Noticing this, Ded Prokop gave me a wink and nodded toward his bowl, offering me a try. So, with Grandmother still looking the other way, I took a spoonful. I knew that shchi is lukewarm, so not fearing to burn my mouth, I swallowed everything. It was like a fire had swept through my mouth. I gasped, I coughed, I choked. Grandmother turned from the stove to look at me. Tears were coming out of my eyes. I did not give Ded away, but she knew what had happened.

"What's this you are doing to a small child? Playing your jokes, you old fool . . ."

Ded Prokop sat there, unperturbed, as if he didn't hear her. Leisurely, he continued to drink his fiery shchi.

From then on, whenever we sat down to dinner, Ded Prokop winked at me, offering to treat me to his shchi, but I was no longer curious. Later I learned that Ded Prokop used to grate several red peppers into his bowl, letting the shchi stand till dinner.

I can't tell you how many times he got me. I would swear to myself that I would never trust him, but I could never predict when he would strike. So I wouldn't trust him on five occasions, but would let my guard down on the sixth. And that's when he would get me.

He was the type of man from whom you don't expect a practical joke. His serious exterior had fooled many people.

GRANDMOTHER, Aunt Domna, and her three children used to live in a sod house. After the war there were many such houses in Lokhmotka, other villages, and even in Barabinsk. They weren't temporary dugouts but permanent houses put together with thick layers of dirt and sod and with earthen floors, which on holidays were washed and evened out with a mixture of clay and manure.

I spent my summers in that house. There were other temporary residents besides me: a hen with chickens, which lived under the stove, where most folks keep stove tools.

The stove was attached to wooden bunks—the upper one was for sleeping, the same one for the children and the old folks. The furniture was homemade: a table and benches in the kitchen, a bed and a couple of stools on the other side of the partition, in the front room. Also on the walls, framed or simply glued to newspapers, were photographs of relatives.

Everything was simple, no extras. It was spacious, too, not like nowadays. It was only after the burial of Joseph Stalin, the Leader of All Nations and the Best Friend of All Kolkhozniki, that the village began to indulge in accumulating worldly goods.

As I recall the poverty of our village, I try to understand just how unavoidable it was that the nation's providers lived in such horrible poverty. True, after the war there was a labor shortage in the village. The men had been killed off. Still, one way or another, the village continued to feed the nation, giving away all it produced—and starving. It was not fair, but it may have been unavoidable. Because of those "unavoidable sacrifices," it wasn't till 1955 that the peasants were able to replace their homespun pants with store-bought ones. Another ten years passed, and they managed to buy bicycles; and now, another decade or so later, they are buying motorcycles and pianos and dreaming about owning cars.

Could it be that the government, in its wisdom, has always known the needs of the people better than the people themselves? So it was decided: "Let Vanya the peasant run around with his gut swelled, but in the future, his children will ride around in an automobile."

But these sacrifices notwithstanding, to this day the country has shortages of meat, butter, and cars. We are buying bread from America and paying for it with our natural resources, "the people's riches."

I am not one to ponder the potential of the Soviet economy and the best avenues for its development. But isn't it common knowledge that many other countries bankrupted by the war were able to revive their economies and, in fact, take them to a much higher level than ours? They did this without "unavoidable sacrifices," without referring to the life of deprivation as "heroism and dedication." That means our sacrifices were senseless after all.

An enormous birch tree, visible from afar, greeted us at the entrance to Lokhmotka. At night it looked like a giant extending his wind-mangled arms either to welcome the traveler to the village—or to scare him off. That giant used to frighten me when I was a child.

Grandmother's *izba* was second from the edge. Nobody lived there anymore. Grandmother had died, and Aunt Domna and the children had moved to Frunze. Nobody wanted the old sod house. People were building normal, wooden houses, abandoning the old earthen ones. So there it stood, its windows broken, gaping holes for doors; even the garden plot had been abandoned.

We went straight to Lyolka's house.

Lyolka and I were happy to see each other after all those years. At a table, which was immediately set and crowned with a bottle, we remembered the relatives, the living, the dead, and the newborn. Lyolka's two daughters have long been married, and she's a grandmother many times over. ("And you're evading!") She works as a cook for a brigade of Armenian *shabashniki* workers hired by the kolkhoz at market rates. The brigade is spending its second summer in the village, doing construction. They are building a cow barn. By the fall, they hope to get a lot of money, and no doubt they will. At the very least it will be ten times what the kolkhoz workers would have been paid for the same work. But the kolkhoz is barely able to handle its work in the fields, so it has to spend a lot of money to get construction workers from the outside.

At the time I visited Lokhmotka, shabashnik brigades were working in virtually every village in our area. In another village, on the way back to Barabinsk, shabash-niki were building a grain dryer. Those guys didn't come from far away. They were young engineers from Novo-sibirsk, each of whom took a month's vacation plus a two-week leave of absence, during which they earned roughly half of an engineer's annual salary.

My cousin's husband is a manager in that village. "I've had it with them," he lamented.

Every morning he and the brigade leader had to go from house to house to cajole or threaten the women to come out and milk the cows. It didn't always work, and it happened that the cows weren't milked till dinner.

"Perhaps you don't pay those women enough," I suggested.

"Don't we? We pay no less than two hundred rubles a month!" He was indignant. "There used to be a time when they tilled from dawn to dusk for a handful of grain, and it didn't take no threats to get them out. They'd run on their own. And now you have to bow to every one of them individually! And we take them to and from work by auto, when it used to be that they'd stay in the fields a week at a time."

"So you want it to be like in the past? A handful of grain?"

"That's not the point. They are getting paid, all right. There's money for them, as long as they want to work. But they don't want to. No one's in charge anymore!"

"You want Stalin, right?"

"And what was wrong with Stalin? At least everything functioned with him around. Life stunk, but people were obedient."

"Are your bosses longing after Stalin, too? People like you used to walk a tightrope, too. So why can't you think of something other than Stalinism to pull the economy out of neutral?"

"So you want capitalism again? Is that what you mean? Huh?"

He never did make a place for himself in Socialist agriculture. He left that *sovkhoz*, then another. Eventually, he left the land and took a safer, less risk-filled position in some bureaucracy.

IN THE VILLAGE, as in Barabinsk, no one asked me what I had been in for, with whom, and what the camps were like.

Only one relative, already soused, picked up another bottle of samogon and beckoned me outside. "We have to talk."

Unable to find a place for our talk outside, he took me to the bath, poured himself a glass, drank up, and asked: "Tell me, is it true, what everyone's saying, that you've sold yourself?"

"To whom? How do they tell it?"

"To foreign intelligence services!"

"Well, if they say foreign intelligence, then it's true."

"What did you sell yourself for? Your grandfather was shot here by Kolchak! And your father went through the war."

"They pay well. Real well. They'd never pay this well for honest labor here."

"And what if they catch you?"

"They aren't doing it anymore. What's with you?

69

Who needs it, catching spies? That's just for books and movies."

"They don't try you for espionage?" His bottle froze over the glass as he stared at me.

"Well, look at me. I am alive and I'm at large."

"Does the KGB know?"

"About what? About me being at large or about me being a spy?"

"About you being a spy."

"Definitely."

"And how do you know that they know?"

"Well, you told me yourself that everyone's saying it. And if everyone's saying it, then the KGB must have known it before everyone else."

He put the bottle and the glass aside, then half whispered, "And what about you? Going against your own people, your own country."

"Well, you see, I had a craving for meat."

"What's meat got to do with it?"

"Everything. Meat's what it's all about. See, spies are paid in foreign currency or in kind. So you walk into a special store for foreigners, and there's everything your soul desires, and no lines, and cheap. And all the meat you want."

He stopped to think, then smiled. "You liar. I come to talk to you seriously, and you . . ."

"How can I talk about it seriously? Everyone says I am a spy, while state security folks are standing by, watching, listening, and doing nothing. How can you talk seriously?"

"How should I know? I hear folks talk, so I come up and ask you, as a relative."

"That's right, folks do the talking and you spread out your ears."

"So what were you in for? Your mother said you were in with the politicals."

"Exactly, I was with them."

"Are there lots of them?"

"More than ten thousand, I guarantee."

"You mean, like under Stalin?"

"No, under Stalin there were millions."

"Still, it's a lot. What are they in for?"

"Different things. Some for books . . ."

"You mean writers? No fooling . . ."

"Some are writers."

"And I thought all writers were whores."

"Not all of them, it turns out."

"Who else is there?"

"There are students. Some of them spoke up at meetings, some wrote leaflets, some put organizations together, set up programs. There are some who are in for the war."

"Those are the ones who ought to be shot. Traitors."

"There are traitors, too. But there are some who fought the Nazis, and the Soviets, too."

"Like *Banderovtsy*.* They are no better."

"What have they done to you?"

"They were shooting us in the back."

"Tell me, did the Ukrainians take Moscow by force, or was it the other way around?"

Finally, completely cross-eyed on samogon, my interlocutor lashed out at America: "You think we won't beat the shit out of America? You bet we will. It's too bad Stalin didn't listen to Zhukov and declare war in nineteen forty-five!"

---

*Anti-Soviet guerrilla forces particularly active in Western Ukraine during World War II and until the 1950s. (Trans.)

It's a popular story, which must have been born in the heat of the final defeat of Germany and the triumph of Soviet armed forces.

"What has America done to you?"

"It's waiting to take us over, that's what."

I didn't want to explain that if America had wanted to take Russia in 1945, it could have done it. Now it couldn't, even if it wanted to. Now I probably would have cautioned him against annexing America to the Socialist Bloc through military action, or even peaceably. If that happened, who would feed us in our years of bad harvests or, for that matter, years of good harvests? Where would we get credits for building socialism? From Ethiopia? From Kim Il Sung?

7

By the early summer of 1967, I left Barabinsk to get a place closer to Moscow.

Six months before, my friends, talking me out of crossing the Soviet border, had convinced me to write the stories the way I told them. So I took the risk of doing the writing myself. Before that, I thought writing was the easiest work around. You make up what you want to write, then keep an eye on the grammar. I didn't even have to make anything up.

In Barabinsk, I had jotted down a few vignettes and mailed them to Moscow. But I could tell that things weren't working out. Everything seemed blurred, vanishing into the ocean of details. I didn't know what to keep and what to leave out. I was spinning in a vicious circle; I felt that I was repeating myself, yet didn't know how to stop. Writing had made me a nervous wreck; still, nothing worked. How should I begin the story? How should I end it? There had to be a place to start, a "once upon a time" of some sort, but I couldn't find it.

By the time I returned to Moscow, my self-confidence was gone. Earlier, Larisa had shown my letters to a few friends, and they kept advising: "Write as best you can." Larisa and I sat down to look over my text and, as a result, my three bulky letters—no fewer than thirty notebook pages—were cut down to five pages. She began by

making me get rid of my declarations against camp regime and the regime as a whole. Those seemed to account for most of my tract. I thought that I had to call
things by their own names, the harsher the better.
"There's absolutely no one who needs this; nobody's interested," Larisa would say. "You must supply the facts,
and let the reader think what he will." I argued with her,
thinking that she was softening up the book for my
safety's sake.

At first I simply had to conform: she had volunteered
to help, so I couldn't ignore her. Later, as I was rereading
the parts of the manuscript that she didn't cross out, I
came close to conceding that she might have been right.
Still, deep inside, I remained defiant, and as I kept writing, I rarely resisted the temptation to hit the reader with
all I had, just as we used to do in run-ins with camp
authorities and visiting lecturers. "You aren't writing for
them," Larisa objected, once again crossing out the offending passages. It was only after B told me that he
agreed with Larisa that I finally accepted that the reader
would do just fine without my cues.

Larisa kept asking questions: How did this and that
happen? What happened afterward? How do I explain
this situation? "That's what you need to add." I kept
making additions, and the text was beginning to take
shape.

From the editing of those first pages I learned that
sentences must be kept simple, as if they were spoken,
and that it's wrong to attempt to squeeze everything you
want to say into one phrase, as if it were your last opportunity to express yourself. I didn't just understand
this; I saw it. I've been trying to write like that since,
though not always succeeding.

In short, the work itself was my source of bravery. Besides, I hoped that, regardless of the quality of my writing, my volunteer editor would make it into something tolerable. That wasn't how it worked out. Larisa didn't do any rewriting: she made me do it. She did, however, cross out parts of phrases, paragraphs, and entire scenes.

The manuscript grew in volume, though very slowly. And all the work I had managed to finish by the end of the summer was yet to fall together into one whole.

Meanwhile, my living conditions turned writing into a hurdle race. Naturally, I could not live in Moscow. There were friends who would have been happy to give me a place to stay, but there was no way I would be able to get a job and a residency permit. Lyuda Alexeyeva helped me rent a place in the Vladimir oblast, about two hours by train from Moscow. With great difficulty I managed to get a residency permit and a porter's job at a liquor and vodka plant. Altogether, getting a job and a residency permit took a month and a half.

I was renting a place from an old lady on the edge of town. Aunt Nyura treated me well, especially after realizing that I was indeed not a drunk and that I didn't mind carrying water from the well, stacking firewood, bringing in peat briquettes. But the job and the chores were taking nearly all of my time.

What's more, I lived in the same room with the landlady. It was a one-room house with a peasant stove in the middle. The area in front of the stove was referred to as "the kitchen"; the area behind it was Aunt Nyura's and my living quarters. She gave me a wooden bed with a straw mattress, and partitioned off my corner with a cupboard and a curtain. Besides the bed, I could fit a chair, on which I set up a suitcase with my laundry, and a small cabinet with dishes and kitchen provisions.

Where could I write? Where could I keep the manuscript?

Whenever I stayed up late, in the morning Aunt Nyura invariably asked: "Tolik, why don't you sleep nights? Your lights were on till dawn, just about."

I could tell her I was writing a letter. That would work once or twice. And then what?

Early on, I lived in a summer addition, basically a porch. I told her that I liked sleeping in fresh air, and I lived there till September. On my days off, I would hide a couple of notebooks in my pockets and go off to the woods "for a walk." But the fall came, and with it, the rains. I had to stop my "walks" in the forest and take my lawful place behind the curtain. Meanwhile, I had to hurry. More than anything else, I feared that the authorities would somehow get wind of my literary pursuits and put me away under any pretext. It's no problem to cook up some "criminal case" in Aleksandrov. So my work would not get done, and I'd wind up in the camps for nothing. I didn't think I would attract attention, but I kept getting visits from Larisa and other Muscovites who were on the KGB watch list. I visited those people in Moscow, too. There was no way to avoid that. What if they showed up in my absence and combed through my modest belongings? Or what if Aunt Nyura became curious about what I was writing at night? Who knows, she could get scared and report me. I took all my notebook pages to work, but what if they fell out of my pockets?

The experiences of my camp colleagues demonstrated that any criminally punishable act should be carried out in a single bound, otherwise you get burned with nothing accomplished. I had to move fast, very fast.

Larisa, too, didn't have the time to devote to my rough drafts. She worked during the week, and when she came over on weekends, she was so tired that she fell asleep almost immediately after sitting down to edit.

8

AT LAST I got a lucky break.

An acquaintance of mine got a room at a retreat for people in the arts. Since it was fall, there was hardly anyone there, about five or six people living in the cabins. Some of them showed up only on Sundays, so on weekdays the place was nearly deserted. My acquaintance rented a large room, and she, too, came only on weekends. She offered the room to me and made the necessary arrangements with the administrator. No one knew me there, and at that retreat spending days writing was not regarded as suspicious behavior.

Fortunately, the liquor-vodka plant gave me a two-month leave of absence. Larisa, too, took her vacation.

So there we were, at the retreat. The grounds were wooded, and the tall fence didn't cut the place off from the outside world; there were plenty of holes, which could be used to exit in any direction, without making a detour through the main gate. About ten minutes away, in the village, there was a diner, where one could get a cheap meal every day.

It so happened that the place was exceptional for mushrooms, and that year they were unusually plentiful. We didn't have to go far to pick them. They grew, literally, on the other side of the fence. That, too, was a lucky break: we boiled those mushrooms; we fried them; for two weeks we ate nothing but mushrooms.

On Sundays, when our friend came, we allowed ourselves a little rest. The three of us took long walks and, at night, made bonfires. It was a pleasure to take a break, to spend a few hours throwing brushwood in the fire, jabbering about everything in the world.

Otherwise, we spent about eighteen hours a day over the manuscript. Every evening, dissatisfied and more tired than a dog, I pushed the manuscript aside. Physical labor never left me this exhausted. I still could not see whether the book worked; I still couldn't see the end. Those two weeks were my last chance. After that I'd be back to the plant, back to the chores, back to my curtained-off corner. Almost a year had passed since my release; another year could pass the same way, fruitlessly; then the KGB could catch the scent, and I'd be done for. I was tense and angry; I felt that even the time spent at dinner was time squandered, so I tormented Larisa whenever we wasted as much as a minute.

She may have had more work than I. After all, I had a substantial backlog. The time had come to organize my writing, to decide what else it needed. The scenes had to be strung on a single thread. "Why don't you make it your own story?" Larisa suggested. "Introduce yourself, explain how you got to Mordovia, then tell the story as it happened: Vladimir Prison, the camp, what you saw there." I took a sheet of paper and jotted down "My name is Anatoly Marchenko." From there on, everything went smoothly, more or less. Larisa and I had one disagreement. She wanted me to write that I was first arrested *allegedly* for a fight. That story was something I did not want to get into. Larisa started to ask questions, but I didn't want to tell even her. I didn't enjoy explaining that I did not take part in that fight and that I had been railroaded. To begin with, every zek will tell you that he's not guilty. Second, that story would have looked like an attempt to set the record straight. Besides, who cares if I was guilty; who cares if I was innocent; that wasn't what the book was about.

Looking back, I think I was right not to take Larisa's advice. It was good for the book and good all around. Later, when the interrogators were confronting my friends with something like: "Do you know whom you are dealing with? He's a criminal, a bandit, a hooligan," my friends could respond with a clean conscience: "Yes, I know. He wrote about it."

The scenes I had written earlier were being arranged chronologically, lining up one after another, like beads on a string. To my surprise, some of them were being included without editing, short chapters including "The Suicides" and "Flowers in the Compound." Others required Larisa's treatment: she crossed out my declarations, eliminated unnecessary detail, pointed out where there was no beginning and where there was no end. Then I would make the changes. A number of scenes wound up being crossed out altogether. They were repeating what had already been said. I didn't want to throw anything away, not after all the sweat I had poured over every page! I argued, sometimes winning, but generally agreeing in the end.

To this day I regret that we were in such a hurry. That's the reason the last chapters of the book came out so light and thin; they could have used some sitting back and thinking over. When I got to them, I was more rushed than at the start, so, from what I can tell, they came out as superficial. When it came to those chapters, the time pressure was just one of my problems. In them, I describe the last year of my term, 1966, when I got to know a new set of political prisoners, those convicted a year earlier. Among them were some famous people, and I thought that naming them would make it look like I was latching onto their fame. Not mentioning them wasn't appropriate, either (though that was my original intention). Eventually, after consulting with friends, I hazarded to give a fleeting mention to those new cadres of political prisoners, but without pretending to have been in close contact with them and not claiming insight into their inner feelings. I had no such insight. Still, I retained an unpleasant aftertaste, as if I was dropping famous names to promote my book.

When I got out of the camps, I brought out my notes, which only I could understand. They were on a notebook cover—a few last names, a few first names, and a few jumbled sentence fragments. When I was frisked before the release, nobody paid attention to those pages. In short, I had some notes, but the bulk of information was in my memory. It's curious that not long after I wrote everything down, I could no longer recall many details and had forgotten many a name. Just a year after I finished the book, I would have been unable to reconstruct it from memory.

Now, as I recall this, our days at the retreat somehow seem like months. It was only two weeks. And by the end of our "vacation" it turned out that the book was nearly completed. There were about 200 double pages covered in my tight handwriting. The last few pages had been shaped in my mind two or three days before I got to them; it was as if someone had dictated them to me. They didn't have to be changed at all.

A few days later, the three of us—B, Larisa, and I— discussed a few alternatives for the title. They upheld *My*

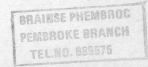

Testimony. It stayed. At that time, with B's help, we put together the introductory pages.

What lay ahead was the final and most urgent phase—typing the manuscript. If we managed to hide just one version, then no matter what happened to me, the work wouldn't be lost. I wouldn't find peace until then.

9

WHILE WE WERE still at the retreat, I gave B a portion
of the manuscript, and he agreed to do the typing. Now
it turned out that he'd finished ten or twenty pages, after
which he stopped. I was furious. He volunteers to do
the work, then leaves me hanging! B defended himself,
saying that it was his wife who wouldn't let him finish.
"I see, you are helping Tolya go to prison," she kept
reproaching him. Now, that's what I call a do-gooder!
And what if an untyped, handwritten, version ended up
in the KGB archives instead of reaching the readers?
Would that be better? It would certainly not ease my
fate. I would be jailed regardless, and if the manuscript
were not made public, it would happen even sooner.

I was furious with B and his wife. I would have to do
the typing myself, though in those days I couldn't type
at all. I'd managed to write something, so I'd type it up,
too—one letter at a time, if that was what it took.

I went to Aleksandrov and quit my job. I would be
jailed soon anyway, so time was what I needed most.

But, once again, my Moscow friends came to the rescue. I managed to convince them that they no longer
had a choice except to "help me go to prison" for a good
cause. Besides, it was October 1967; the fiftieth anniver-
sary of the revolution was coming up, and there were
predictions of a big amnesty. Such rumors spread through
the camps before every big jubilee, and though they

never come true, there is always an element of "perhaps this time . . ." That's part of the human condition. If the book got out before the amnesty, and if that amnesty included the "especially dangerous crimes," a category in which *My Testimony* would put me, then it would be possible that my criminal act would fall under the amnesty. I didn't really believe this. But I think that scenario, more than anything else, convinced my friends that we had to hurry.

We decided on the fastest way to type up the manuscript. The T——s, who had an apartment of their own, offered that the work be done at their place. They procured three typewriters, so the four people among us who could type worked in shifts. Those who could not type dictated to them, stacked up the carbon copies, and corrected typos. One couple with a typewriter worked in the kitchen, another worked in one of the rooms. The hosts' child slept in the room between them. The tapping resonated throughout the apartment, and it may have been heard at the neighbors' as well. Heaps of blank paper, carbons, and manuscript pages were stacked all around. In the kitchen someone was constantly making coffee and sandwiches, and, at any given time, at least one of us was asleep on the couch or on a cot. We worked for two days straight, taking turns sleeping, not distinguishing day from night.

A few of those who came to help had just learned about the book and were yet to read it. Yu and our host, T, immediately sat down to read.

From time to time, T, a hot-tempered, emphatic man with a tendency to exaggerate, jumped up, and with appropriate hand gestures, declared: "If Galina Borisovna [a fictional character whose initials, G.B., were his nickname for the KGB] knew what's being typed here, she would bring a division and surround the whole square block!" As he read, he suggested revisions, and when I accepted them without arguing, he exclaimed, "Way to go, old man. You're accepting it all. Just like Leo Tolstoy." Yu was also suggesting changes. He couldn't stay the whole time, so he read only a few chapters. "I think this is more powerful than an A-bomb," he said as he was leaving. I didn't take these hastily rendered critiques seriously, but I did realize that my book was accomplishing its goal.

By dawn of the third day the work was done, and with a suitcase filled with rough drafts and ready copies, we left the apartment. One copy remained with our hosts, for reading and safekeeping.

The streets were still deserted, and there wasn't a trace of Galina Borisovna. Before going to Larisa's, we decided to stop over at K and T's. Those people were dear to us (subsequently, we became close friends). We called them from a phone booth. "Can we come over?" It wasn't even 6:00 A.M. yet. "Right now? Certainly." The sleepy hosts opened the door and took us to the kitchen; the children were still asleep in the room.

"Would you mind hiding this manuscript really well for a while?" Larisa asked.

"Of course not."

I did not suggest that they read the book. That way, if the KGB happened to catch them with the manuscript, they would be able to say that they knew nothing about it, and that they were simply doing me a favor— and that wouldn't be a lie. It was much later that K and T read the book.

. . .

ONE COPY of the book had to be dispatched to the West, and only after that could the book be allowed to circulate in the Motherland.

The opportunity to get the book to the West soon presented itself. Then came the torture by expectation: I could barely wait to get the word that the book had arrived without a problem. Where would it go? Who would publish it? Those matters didn't worry me in the least. I didn't receive any such word, and for that reason, I kept passing along (personally and through friends) additional copies of the manuscript to the West. To this day I have no idea which of the copies finally made it to the publisher. It was more than a year later that I learned that the book had been published in the West. By that time, I was back in the camps.

After leaving two copies with friends for safekeeping, sending one to the West and three into samizdat, I was left with only one copy, which I wanted to submit to some magazine. There, when they received it, they would stamp it with a date of receipt. Who knows, I could then get lucky and become eligible for amnesty.

Back when I decided to bring to light the conditions in political camps, I didn't count on mercy. I never even thought of such a thing as amnesty. But when the work was behind me, I began to play the guessing game, hoping for a lucky star in my fate.

My Moscow friends, whom I regarded as authorities on literature, had given me favorable critiques of my book. Still, that was a narrow circle of friends, whose judgment, undisputably, was not impartial. I couldn't wait to hear the opinions "from outside," from people who would be able to offer impartial critiques. Early on, when I was just starting to work on the book, it didn't even occur to me to wonder about critiques and opinions. I wanted to give the facts to the public, to alert it to the truth that was being thoroughly hidden from it by the government. That was all. I didn't care about the artistry of prose and what would be said about it. I had one honest response to all criticism I could encounter in that regard: I am not a writer. Now it turned out that an author's vanity was not beyond me.

The comments I was getting were positive, though it could have been that others simply weren't reaching me. Readers were comparing Stalin's camps with the contemporary (many, on the basis of firsthand experience) and concluding that the system hadn't changed. Many said they were astonished by the discovery that political camps of such systematized cruelty could exist in our time. It was also said that the book was well written and that it projected a sense of confidence in the witness's testimony. That, of course, was my goal. "How did it happen that it was you, a common man, who wrote this book? Why hasn't one of us, the intelligentsia, done it first?" fumed L, a just-released zek I knew from Mordovia. He liked the book.

Before my arrest in July 1968, I got two negative comments. One came from a well-known scientist, who said it was possible that the book was accurate, but it was wrong to show prison and the camps in such a horrible light. "It would make people fear arrest," he said.

Aleksandr Solzhenitsyn, I was told, found that today's convicts as I described them appeared too brave, too undaunted by fear of punishment cells and other sanctions. "It doesn't seem believable that this is the way it really happened."

But those comments came later. For now, I showed *My Testimony* to K, a well-known literary scholar. He liked the book a lot.

"What are your plans for it?" he asked.

I said that I had sent it to the West and that now I wanted to send it to some magazine. Then I gave him my reasons.

K personally arranged with the editors of one of the magazines that they would accept the manuscript and keep it in a place where it would not be discovered by any of the known informants.

No more than a week later I was asked to come to that magazine's editorial offices and reclaim the manuscript. It turned out that in that time the book had been read by several employees. They gave high marks to the book and, as I was told, to "the author's courage." The author, they said, "has dared to sacrifice himself, literally, sacrifice his life, but why is he bent on dragging others behind him? In the end, our magazine would suffer as well." Naturally, I immediately took the manuscript back, though I was not too clear about the cause of suffering for the magazine that had accepted an unknown manuscript from an unknown author and had *not* published it. Later I was told that the magazine was bound by some written or unwritten laws which mandate that seditious manuscripts like mine be routed to the KGB. So the decent people at that magazine did not want to become informants, but they were also afraid to keep the book. They didn't even register its receipt.

It's unfortunate that those people, in their fear for the magazine, were prepared to accuse me of the insincere, deceitful strategy of trying to implicate the magazine's editors in the act of distributing the book by making it seem that the book had been launched into samizdat from their editorial offices. It could be that they had had dealings with such dishonorable authors. I don't know if they believed me that nothing of the sort had ever crossed my mind, and that I had no intentions of dragging decent people down with me; I wouldn't do that even to a lowlife. It was all the more difficult to explain myself because all negotiations were conducted through third parties. My direct involvement was limited to returning to pick up the manuscript, and when I did, I sensed no ill will. "We read your account with great excitement," I was told, and as I was leaving, I was offered an apple. (That was my second honorarium for the book. The first honorarium, or more precisely, an advance, came to me in the woods behind the retreat clubhouse: in the thick grass, where there were no signs of man, I bent over to pick up a mushroom, and found a ten-ruble bill. It was wet and wrinkled, like a battered leaf in the fall, but it was still fit for use. I spent it on a pair of vinyl boots.)

AN APPLE in my hand, a manuscript under my arm, I headed for the editorial offices of *Moskva* magazine, a place where, I was assured, no one would be distressed by having to inform the KGB, so I did not need to worry about dragging anyone down with me. No one recommended me to the *Moskva* editors, so to them I was just a man from the street. From this day—November 2, 1967—on, it all would turn like a whirlpool.

Here is Arbat. The *Moskva* offices are to the right of the metro.

"Why is the copy so poor?" asks the secretary, recording the particulars on an index card. There is displeasure but no animosity in her voice. I mutter something in response. They got the last carbon rather than the one I picked up at the other magazine. It will do, it will do, they'll manage. The convenience of those to whom this book will be forwarded from here is the least of my worries.

"What is it? A novel? A story?"

I haven't given that a thought. Call it a story.

"Fictional or documentary?"

Documentary, of course. "Documentary."

The secretary takes down the information and slides the manuscript into a desk drawer without so much as glancing at the title page.

"Come back in about a month to get the reply. Or the reply could be mailed to you."

Where will my manuscript be in a month? And where will I be?

ALL OF MY FRIENDS were concerned about my fate. At first, they advised me to publish the book under a pseudonym and not slip it in to any magazines. How many arguments we had over it! There were group discussions and discussions with individuals; there were debates that erupted spontaneously at home, and there were carefully orchestrated nighttime strolls. The predictions were the same: "They won't forgive you for this." Some ventured to forecast the forms of retribution: from a closed court proceeding ("Then they knock you off in the camps") to my "accidental" murder in a street fight or in an accident. Those grim predictions said a lot about the way the people, including the intelligentsia, viewed the KGB— and about the reputation that organization had created for itself by 1967.

It was sober calculation rather than uncommon valor that made me reject the idea of using a pseudonym. *My Testimony* describes specific places, people, and events

during a specified period. All this would give the "interested parties" enough to go on to determine the book's true author. That's not to mention that there's no such thing as testimony under a pseudonym.

After I submitted the manuscript to *Moskva*, and after the ukase on amnesty (which, as could have been expected, did not include the politicals), my friends and even people I barely knew made attempts to convince me to go into hiding. I remember N spent two hours walking me up and down the courtyard (such conversations were held outside; we feared the apartments were under electronic surveillance), trying to convince me to hop a train for the Northern Caucasus, where her husband had friends who could hide me. "Don't you understand? They'll just knock you off! Who needs your heroism! It doesn't impress anyone!" I. had found me a reliable hideout and, if I am not mistaken, even a job somewhere in the southwest; K was offering a safe place somewhere in the Arkhangel'sk oblast. Everyone agreed on one point: that I should not return to Aleksandrov, not even to pick up my things. There I would be knocked off on the first night.

The idea of going underground didn't appeal to me. First of all, when they started looking (and I know how it's done) they would launch a nationwide search, and, most likely, would find me sooner or later. In that sense, Aleksandrov was no worse than any of the "safe places" offered to me. Second, I had submitted my written testimony and wanted to reserve the right to confirm it in person. "Here I am, the very same Anatoly Marchenko. Who says *My Testimony* is a fake?" Of course, it would be desirable to remain on the outside as long as possible, long enough for the book to be published and become well known; that would make the authorities think twice before arresting me. It might force them to control their predatory drive.

So I didn't return to Aleksandrov; I tried to get a place in Moscow where I could stay out of their sight. I found work, though not of the paying variety. I decided to retype my book—and learn to type in the process. The first batch of copies was gone, and my own copy had perished tragically: I gave it to a friend, a good man who had done a lot for me, and he got spooked (it turned out falsely) and, as a precaution, burned the manuscript.

Now I wasn't in a hurry. Friends were supplying me with books. I was preparing for my impending arrest and trial. I wrote my "Last Word" statement to the court, memorized it, and gave a copy to friends. The trial would be closed, so this would be the only way to find out what I said. My other concern was to find a "relation" among my Moscow friends, so that after the arrest that person would be able to file petitions, make arrangements with the defense attorney, demand to visit me in prison. One fine—and unmarried—friend, Ira Belogorodskaya, enlisted as my "fiancée." We filed a marriage application, so our "relationship" was properly documented.

I lived calmly through early December. Perhaps no one was looking for me yet, or perhaps they couldn't find me (that was unlikely since I wasn't hiding), or it could have been that they were watching and I hadn't noticed.

10

LARISA AND HER SON, Sanya Daniel, went off on a visit to Mordovia, and I asked to stay in their apartment and take care of the dog.

So here I am, in a vacant apartment, slowly pecking away on the typewriter. Suddenly, I get a feeling that someone is fiddling with the window. Since I work with my hearing aid out, I don't hear them; I guess. Abruptly, I pull the curtain. Outside is a well-fed and well-groomed young man, dressed ceremonially, as if he were returning from a diplomatic reception. Another one is at a distance, lurking behind a tree. Unlike the first, he is unkempt and disheveled.

"Open the door!"

"Are you coming in through the window?"

"*Otkroyte!*"—Open up!

"The hosts aren't home. Without them, I am not letting anyone in. That goes double for anyone breaking in through the window."

"Open the door!"

"Sure thing. Who are you?"

"You are being told, open the door!"

"Who are you?"

Slowly, unwillingly, he reaches into the breast pocket of his black coat, pulls out a red identification booklet, and shows me its outside jacket. I read the gold script on red background, under a gold coat of arms: THE COMMIT-

A thought flashes: "Well, it's begun." I had been expecting an encounter with that organization. Here it is.

The *gebeshnik* is holding his ID against the glass, apparently counting on its hypnotizing effect. I open the window a tad, lean toward him, then say, "Now take your ID and get the hell out of here."

I shut the window. The gebeshnik makes an unsuccessful attempt to keep me from locking the frame. I read his lips: *"Otkroyte"*—Open up. "You are being told."

I draw the curtain and, feverishly, start running around the room gathering up pages and carbons. I decide to burn it all in the toilet. I throw the heap in the commode, then start running around the kitchen in search of matches. There are none to be found. The night before, Sanya and Larisa took the last box off the stove. I was to go out and get a new box in the morning. But I didn't go out; I used the neighbor's matches, then returned the box to him. No matches; now that's a good one.

The doorbell rings incessantly. It's them. I fear that Pavel Ilych, the neighbor, will walk out and open up. I know he is in his room, but for some reason he is not coming out.

I run to the bathroom and, to the ceaseless sounds of the doorbell, start tearing each sheet in four, then flushing, watching the water rush the "evidence" into oblivion. I tear up a few more, but there is no water: it takes some time for the tank to fill! This way I'll need at least an hour; and they won't wait. They'll break the door. Or Pavel Ilych will get his fill of their ringing and open up.

I try to think: let's say they take me now, then no one will know. (Pavel Ilych, if I read him correctly, will do what he is doing now, act as if nothing has happened.) They will also get all of my papers; on top of that, I have a copy of Djilas's *The New Class* and the works of Tertz and Arzhak.* The KGB would gladly hang this evidence of "sedition" on Larisa; their teeth are set for her as it is. My explanation: I was left in the apartment to take care of the dog. The hosts didn't know what I was going to do there; I didn't tell them. If only I could convince Larisa to confirm this version! She has to be warned. I must see her.

I run out of the bathroom, leaving behind a stack of typewritten pages. I throw on a coat, get my feet into shoes (there's no time to lace them up), grab my passport (my last fifteen rubles are in it), and lunge for the window. Carefully, I look out from behind the curtain. There are no signs of the "diplomat," but the other, the disheveled one with a bandit's face, is out there, at some distance. I notice him looking out from behind a bush. He hasn't moved, the bastard; still watching the window.

I go to the other room, carefully open the window. It overlooks a small yard fenced off with a chain-link fence, about 2 meters high. I look out. As always, there isn't a soul around. I jump out and, as fast as I can, run along the building toward the street. I reach the chain-link fence, and in an instant, I am on top. Looking back for the first time, I see the bandit-faced gebeshnik scurrying around. He sees me all right, but it's too late.

I jump off the fence and run toward a trolley stop.

_____

*Pseudonyms for the Soviet dissident writers Andrei Sinyavsky and Yuli Daniel. (Trans.)

Just as I hop onto a departing trolley and hear the door close behind me, I see the gebeshniki run out of the archway and nervously rush about among the passersby.

At the next stop, I get off and run into a courtyard. Through adjoining courtyards, I make my way to an open-air market, where there are lots of people and lots of pay phones. I have to tell someone I know about what has happened. I dial. There is an answer—thank God! I squeeze the whole story into a couple of words and hear:

"Come on over. Or we can come and get you."

AFTER GETTING to that friend's house, I started to think over what had happened and what needed to be done. Now, with the friends warned and able to tell Larisa everything, I thought of returning to the apartment, to see what was going on there.

"It's no secret what's happening there. A search! And there's nothing for you to do there," my friends protested. "What an idea, going up there. Let *them* find you; that's what they get paid for."

Ira Belogorodskaya and a friend went to Larisa's apartment instead of me. To everyone's surprise they found everything the way I'd left it: the typewriter out of its case, the papers thrown around the room, torn pages piled up by the toilet, the unlocked window. The neighbor was walking through this chaos, apparently oblivious to it. It seemed no one had been in the apartment. Why not? That remains a mystery.

Ira and her friend put everything in order and left, taking with them the evidence of my criminal activity. The puzzling conduct of the KGB left us wondering: Why did they come? Whom did they want? Larisa or me?

All the same, Larisa had to be warned before her return to Moscow.

So I decided to go after her and meet up with her on her way back, in Pot'ma or Yavas. I was being dissuaded, but I so badly wanted to see her once more before they threw me back in the camps.

11

I COULD NOT demonstrate rationally the necessity of my trip, and my friends attributed it all to khokhol stubbornness: "Marchenko cannot be swayed." That established, they did their best to help me.

First, I had to be given a more or less decent pair of trousers: I'd jumped out of the window as I was, wearing satin pants with a gaping hole in the knee. Finding a pair of untorn spare pants in that circle was no easy matter. Still, a pair was found, significantly larger than what I normally wear.

To keep me from pacing around at the station, a friend sent her son to get the ticket. He got one at a student rate, and gave me his student identification as proof. He did so realizing that if I happened to get caught with his ID, he would be thrown out of his graduating class. To my shame, I realized that only the next day, when I was densely surrounded by a detachment of gebeshniki, who accompanied me even to the railroad car bathroom. After getting away from them, and locking myself up in the bathroom, I ripped the student ID into small shreds and, one after another, dispatched them through the crapper hole, to freedom. My "escort" was banging on the door. Having disposed of the document, I thought, "And what if I hadn't managed to do it?"

Of course, that trip to Mordovia was a harebrained venture, which didn't have a glorious end. In Pot'ma, after all, every dog (in uniform) knew me. It so happened that the first person I ran into was Afanasyev, the official in charge of reeducation at Camp 11. He recognized me from afar, despite my "civilian" look and my Charlie Chaplin pants. Could it be that they had been expecting me? Immediately, Afanasyev ran to the camp administration office. Minutes later I was confronted by Major Postnikov, head of the KGB at Dubrovlag, the administrative unit that ran all twenty camps in Mordovia, and Captain Krut, the KGB officer at Camp 11. I had been released from that camp a year earlier. The conversation was to the point: "You get on the first train out; there's nothing for you here."

"And what if I don't go?" I objected for appearances' sake.

"Then, Marchenko, we'll give you fifteen days' detention for hooliganism. And while you're there, we'll find you something more suitable. Something to put you away for three to seven."

Indeed, there was nothing for me there; not after they caught up with me. It meant I had to wait for Larisa and Sanya at the railroad station in Pot'ma.

But in Pot'ma, once again, I saw Afanasyev.

"Why don't you get your ticket to Moscow, Marchenko, and get the fuck out of here?"

"Get away from me!" I snapped. "You mean nothing to me here. Nor I to you."

"Don't you forget what Postnikov promised you!"

I looked around. There were six men with him. They took me in a circle, walked me to the ticket office, and from there, without a ticket (none were available), to the just-arrived train.

"Don't even think of staying! You can get there, ticket or no ticket."

Then they pushed me inside the car, with a crowd of other stowaways. Perhaps all they wanted was for me to leave. But after the train left Pot'ma, I noticed that my escort had stayed on. At the next station, some of them, including Afanasyev, got off, to be replaced by another detail; they were passing me from hand to hand. In Ryazan, trying to get away, I jumped out just as the train was about to move. All hell broke loose: the entourage, more numerous than I imagined, jumped out of both doors, jumped on top of me, twisted my arms, and pushed me back into the already moving train. I screamed to the passersby: "Look! This is the KGB! The KGB is grabbing a man! I am coming back from the Mordovian camps for politicals!"

People stopped, crowded around, but didn't get involved. The gebeshniki, nonetheless, thought it necessary to explain themselves: "We aren't any KGB; just regular passengers. Here's my driver's license. I am a chauffeur. Here."

"So why did you grab me?"

"Calm down, comrade, you are mentally ill. We must deliver you to a hospital."

So, is this the arrest? If it is, it's a strange one: I seem to be traveling on my own, but not freely, and under guard.

It was at that moment that I destroyed the student ID: first I kneaded it to pulp in my pocket, then I flushed it down the toilet.

Then, taking advantage of my unusual travel arrangements, lying on my upper bunk, I wrote a few notes to Larisa, then threw them over to other passengers. I saw them pick up the notes, but, as I found out later, no one delivered them to her address. That was how I whiled away the hours on the trip back to Moscow.

At the railroad station I was met by a few men in plain clothes and uniformed militia; my Mordovian guard detachment handed me over to them. The Moscow detachment picked me up off the railroad car steps and dragged me off, calming me down with "Easy now, easy, let's not have any resistance."

I screamed as loudly as I could about the KGB and the Mordovian camps. All the while, they kept punching me in the ribs and kicking me in the legs.

Let me explain: I did not scream out of fear or out of an excess of emotion. I screamed for a reason. Sometime earlier, my friends and I had talked about the intelligentsia acting too intelligentsialike in confrontations with the authorities. They are grabbed by both arms and told ever so calmly, *"Proydemte"*—We need to talk, or "Follow us, quietly." And the *intelligent* follows silently, not even inquiring whom he is following, why, and under what authority. He would never pull away or try screaming; that would be embarrassing, awkward.

For the KGB, it's a convenience. They can pick up a man in the street, with no one turning his head. No one notices a thing; there is no unnecessary noise, no disturbance. So the hell with them, it might have been awkward for me, but I'd make it awkward for them, too! I am not an *intelligent*, so I'd survive this embarrassment one way or another.

They kicked and dragged me all through the station, took me someplace around the corner, then to the second floor, then into a room; they seated me in a chair, flanked on both sides by plainclothesmen. Of course, I stopped screaming; there was no longer an audience.

I sat and waited; now they would show me the arrest warrant and take me to prison. Suddenly a man in plain clothes walked in and said: "Anatoly Tikhonovich, it's a

little early. The supervisory personnel are not in yet."
(When has it ever been too "early" to drag a man to
prison?) "There is no one here to chat with you," he
continued.

Chat? What chat? A search, then the *voronok* prison van.

"You are free to go now, but please return by around
ten A.M.," he continued.

Was this a dream? I was so disoriented that, foolishly,
I said, "I won't return in the morning. I won't return
in the evening. You grab me, drag me around, God knows
what for. Some blasted chat."

Then I came to my senses and, without delay, ran out
of the office, then into the street, still not fully believing
that they'd let me go. Could they be playing with me,
like a cat with a mouse? I kept waiting for them to stop
me: "Hey, Marchenko! Where do you think you are going?" Could it be that they hadn't dispensed with all the
formalities? As soon as they did, they'd catch up and
throw me behind bars, I concluded.

I ran to the pay phone to call someone as quickly as
possible, while I was still free. I called N.P., waking her
up. She was delighted. "Catch a taxi and rush over here."

There I was, speeding through the deserted streets of
predawn Moscow, still not fully believing that I was free.

Meeting N.P. was one of the best things that had happened in my life since my release from Mordovia—and
to this day. She is a woman of extraordinary kindness,
always coming to the aid of anyone she knows who needs
help. She even seeks out such people. N.P. does not make
a show of it; she goes about it quietly, even unnoticeably,
answering the call of her soul. And that's what I like best
about her. She doesn't help just political prisoners and
their families. She helps little old ladies, young people,

her distant relatives. And her help is easy to accept; it never gives you a sense of inferiority. N.P. and those she helps have a normal, informal, friendly relationship. She always treated me as part of the family, like a younger brother, and when I was at her place, I felt like I was at the house where I grew up rather than in a sanctuary.

I told her about my adventures, and we both started guessing what the authorities might be up to. After dawn, we called Ira Belogorodskaya and asked her to meet Larisa and Sanya at the railroad station and bring them to N.P.'s. I was afraid they would be bringing some written materials from the camp and, unsuspectingly, get searched. That would be just what they needed!

N.P. didn't have to go to work that day, so she started making breakfast for everyone. Having nothing better to do, I walked out on the staircase. It was either instinct or a sense of foreboding that made me look out the window. From above, there was a clear view of the opposite side of the street, the roadway, and a little park. Normally, this early in the morning, the passersby were rushing to the bus stop. But, looking down, I saw some men unhurriedly walking in the park by N.P.'s doorway, talking to each other and glancing at the doorway. There was a car nearby. Damn, it had to be a black Volga, like in the detective movies. Three or four men in plain clothes were in it, and every now and then the others, those keeping an eye on the doorway, were coming up to them and saying something.

I understood immediately that these were my personal *toptuny*, my very own surveillance team. Had they followed me from the railroad station, or had they intercepted the call? Were they going to wait for me to come out, or were they going to enter the apartment? So it was cat-and-mouse after all. I returned to the apartment; then

N.P., too, walked out to the stairway, looked out, and concurred that it appeared that the doorway was under surveillance.

Soon Larisa and Sanya came by, accompanied by Ira and her friend. Ira told us that at the railroad station she'd noticed they were being followed, and that some car had tailed them from the station, then turned off somewhere along the way.

"It's all right, we have one here," N.P. and I quipped.

After breakfast, N.P. had to run some errands. We decided not to stay in the apartment without the hostess but to walk out with her—and see what happened. But first, N.P. called her brother and asked him to get his movie camera and come over.

Yu.P. is an upstanding citizen; he is a deputy of the regional soviet, a scientist, and a war invalid (he walks on an artificial leg). He was even allowed on business outside the country. Still, he calmly heard his sister out (N.P. just wanted to use his movie camera), then said that he would walk out with us, too. With a friend of N.P.'s who also joined in, there were now eight of us.

WE WALK OUT of the doorway. Instantly, the agents come to life, conduct some sort of a regrouping maneuver, then spread out; the Volga's engine begins to huff. We cross the street, moving toward a taxi stand. We walk slowly; Yu.P. limps. We are followed by a couple of goons who had been stationed at the doorway. One of them, wearing a fur hat, passes us and runs into a bread store. We see him watching us through the window. Larisa walks into a phone booth, and, instantly, he winds up at the adjacent booth, peering in to see what number she is dialing. Without making a call, Larisa walks out; Fur Hat, too, drops the receiver and pops out of the phone booth. There is haste and panic in his eyes, as if he hadn't crammed his lesson and is afraid he'll fail.

Yu.P. mutters: "The audacity . . ."

He takes the camera and directs the lens at the pursuit party. Their attention is focused on those of us walking in front, and since Yu.P. has fallen behind, they don't immediately notice that they are being filmed. When they realize it, they attempt to turn away, even cover their faces with their hands.

When we get to the taxi stand, "our" Volga is already there; it has turned around. Next to it is a hardtop Gazik, which I hadn't noticed earlier. Both cars' antennas are up.

We decide to go to the Byelorussky Railroad Station together. That's where N.P. needs to go. If nothing happens, that's where we would split up. We stop two taxis: N.P., her brother, Sanya, and I get into one; and Larisa, a friend of N.P.'s, and Ira with her friend get into the other. Instantly, the agents jump into their cars, and the entourage is off.

Their Volga is at the head, the taxis behind it, and the Gazik is bringing up the rear. The passengers shift around in their cars, looking at us, talking to each other over the radio. Their cars change places: the first one slows down to let us pass, the other one speeds up, passes us, and takes the place at the head of the procession. At such moments we get to see those people face to face. Naturally, our taxi drivers quickly become aware of the pursuit, and, as it often happens with drivers in such situations, they work up a fervor. They try, unsuccessfully, to pass the first car. (Later I saw many a driver react the same way. Not trying to figure out who was chasing whom and why, they sped up, made abrupt turns, changed direction unexpectedly.)

Yu.P. has his camera out, filming the chase.

Our car gets to the railroad station and slows down near the metro. The black Volga stops, too; the agents file out and take positions around us. The noticeable Fur Hat paces around in front of the station entrance, smoking, not taking his eyes off us. The other car pulls up, the Gazik behind it.

While we settle up with the taxi driver, Sanya walks up to Fur Hat. "Got a smoke?"

He darts away with a hiss. "Get away, get away from here."

It seems strange: they are literally staying on my heels, but they haven't made the arrest. So why are they tailing us? What's the point?

Walking fast, Larisa, Sanya, and I head for the metro (the others in our group walk slower). I put five kopeks in the turnstile, get through, and run down the escalator. The agents lunge after me but neglect to put in their coins (which they may not have had at the ready). The turnstiles lock up. The agents jump over the barrier and, pushing the passengers aside, run downstairs after me. The attendants and the militiaman are appalled by this audacity and run after them. The militiaman is blowing his whistle. I stop to watch this scene from below, waiting for my friends to catch up. Question: Why did I run? Where was I going? I don't really know. It could be that I got caught up in the excitement of the chase.

Larisa, Sanya, and the agents reach me simultaneously. Larisa and Sanya take me by the arms and hold me so I won't be ripped out of their grip. From behind, I hear someone's unpleasant voice mutter: "And where were you running; where were you running?"

The winded metro employees, followed by the militiaman, catch up with us next. The metro people don't care about us; they keep grabbing the offenders by the sleeves, demanding that they follow them upstairs to the militia room. The "offenders" mutter some hazy claims, that they would not take a step without us, that we are all together. The militiaman invites us, too.

"Citizens, proceed upstairs. Let's see what's going on here."

Nothing else to do; we have to follow the servants of law and order. The militia room quickly fills up. There are four agents—they are the "offenders"—and four of us—we are the witnesses—plus several metro employees and the militia. We see Fur Hat take the militiaman aside and whisper something; the militiaman then reports to his boss, the militia officer, glancing at us. The officer nods. After that Fur Hat and the militiaman leave the room, while the officer proceeds with a sluggish and nonsensical line of questioning. It's clear that he is no longer interested in the events at the turnstiles and is simply taking up time, keeping us "occupied." He is waiting for something or someone.

Two men in plain clothes, wearing fedoras, enter the room: one is short and rotund; the other, tall and gaunt. The officer jumps up and offers his chair to the short one, who settles into it like it's his own; you can see which one of them is the boss.

"What's the problem?" the short one asks.

"Those here," says a woman attendant, pointing at the agents. "They impudently ran through the turn-stiles."

"Fine, fine, you return to your post. Is Comrade Officer aware of the situation? He will make a report. You go on, go on."

The officer promptly shows her out.

Then the short one turns to us. "In connection with the incident, you are asked to present your documents."

We realize that they have some sort of a game plan and that it's senseless to argue. Still, we proceed to haggle. These people follow us, we object, they violate public order in the metro, we get detained here because of them, and now we are being ordered to present our documents. Let them present *their* documents.

"Fine, we can start with them. Your documents, please," he says to the agents.

One by one, they hand him employee identifications. He looks through them and reads aloud: "A master at a plant . . . A warehouse employee . . . A metalworker . . . Now, we'll make a note of it. . . ."

"Also make a note of the fact that these masters and metalworkers were chasing us throughout Moscow."

"I didn't chase anybody," says Fur Hat. "I was just going about my business, and accidentally got dragged into this story."

"Accidentally! You and the others, in the same car, accidentally chase us here, then accidentally, all together, run after me into the metro station, then accidentally surround me? And what about jumping over the turnstile without five-kopek coins? Did you do that accidentally?"

"What makes you think that he was following you?" the short one interrupts. "Who are you, actually?"

"And who are you? We don't know you. And you aren't in uniform."

"The two of us, this comrade and I, are from the investigations bureau," says the short one, pointing at his silent, gaunt partner. "My name is Medvedev. We are looking for someone, someone named Marchenko. Could it be that he is among you? Present your documents."

Yu.P. doesn't happen to have any documents, just a card (with a photograph) that entitles him to free use of city transportation, one of the privileges of being a deputy of the city soviet. Medvedev quickly looks through the passports, all except mine. He slows down a bit to ponder Yu.P.'s "deputy pass." On a sheet of paper, he writes down the names of all of my friends, then turns his attention to my passport.

Meanwhile, the tall one, after a whispered conversation with one of the agents, turns to Yu.P.

"Comrade, please open the camera and expose the film."

"Why?" Yu.P. asks.

We, too, chime in. The tall one persists. Medvedev, my passport in hand, is talking with Fur Hat. Then he joins the argument over the movie camera.

"You were conducting filming in the streets of Moscow and in the metro."

"That's not forbidden. We did not even get near any secret sites."

"Expose the film, we are asking you." Once again, Medvedev is doing all the talking, and the tall one stays out.

"I refuse to do so," protests Yu.P. "Why don't you explain what the problem is, why you don't like the movie camera."

"You must expose the film."

"I was among those you filmed," Fur Hat interjects. "And what if I don't like it? Then it's forbidden."

"And what about tailing us? Is that allowed? I don't like that, either."

Medvedev tries to make a joke of it: "Believe me, not everyone likes to be filmed. Take me, for example, I don't like to show off my hairdo in photographs."

With a theatrical gesture, he takes off his fedora and pats his bald scalp.

"We filmed those people because they followed us. The film is our proof."

Jokes aside, the tone now becomes threatening: if you don't voluntarily hand over the camera, we'll take it from you and expose the film. Hearing that, Yu.P. is enraged. The others, seeing that this usually reserved man could, in a fit of fury, say things he would regret later, attempt to calm him down and talk him into conceding. In the end, Yu.P. exposes the film.

Medvedev announces: "Everyone is free to go. Go your own way. As for Marchenko, we need him. Follow us, please," he says, turning to me.

My friends protest: "We won't go anywhere without him. We won't leave him alone with you."

Once again I am held by the arms; the militia can't approach without using force. And they don't want a fight.

"Why are you so distressed over your Marchenko?" Medvedev quips once again, but there is aggravation in his voice. "Nothing is going to happen to him. We'll talk to him; that's all. You've clutched him like we are about to take him from you."

"Let them all walk together if that's what they want," interrupts the tall one. Now it becomes clear that he, not Medvedev, is the real boss.

I try to convince my friends to leave and wait somewhere while we "explain ourselves." But they refuse to listen. All of us come out of the metro and, following

Medvedev and the other one, head toward the militia. The agents are following at a respectful distance.

I am led into an office, while the others wait in the corridor.

In the office, I am pointed to a chair by a desk. Medvedev walks away, as if offering the lead to the tall one, who starts walking slowly around the room. He stops next to me.

"Marchenko, you are consistently in violation of passport regulations. For a long time you have been living in Moscow without a residency permit."

He pauses, as if waiting for me to react to his words. I remain silent. He continues.

"If you do not leave Moscow in the next three days, you will be tried for violation of passport regulations. You are being warned: do not stay in Moscow for over seventy-two hours after this conversation."

Once again, I cannot believe it. Are they letting me go? Could they be? I keep resisting the temptation to ask, "So when are you going to arrest me?" I feel no gratitude to my "liberator."

After a pause, he says, "And another thing, Marchenko, we need to talk to you some more. You know what about."

"Well, talk; I'll listen."

"Not here and not now. Let's agree on a time."

"I don't want to agree with you on anything."

"You will, of course, spend these three days at the Bogoraz apartment? I will call you there and we will make arrangements."

I blow up. It has to be the pressure of the past few days.

"What do you want from me? Tell me. Your boys tail

me, hunt me down, drag me around, and you talk about 'making arrangements,' 'chatting.' If three days is what I've got, I'd rather spend them with friends."

"We have to get together and talk sooner or later, and you, Marchenko, understand it perfectly."

With those words he let me go. I walked out and was surrounded by my friends. Until that minute they didn't believe that I would be let out. They were afraid that the room had a hidden entrance through which, secretly, I would be taken to prison.

12

THAT face-to-face encounter with the KGB, my first, still baffles me. All of my friends were racking their brains over this new and unexpected strategy of the organization that delivers swinging and devastating blows at every opportunity. Everyone had a theory of his own, but they all agreed on one point: that they could not be trusted and that they had cooked up something ruthless and cunning. Once again, I was being advised by my friends to disappear, or, at the very least, not to return to Aleksandrov. Since I was being pressured by the KGB to return there, that was where the greatest danger awaited me, I was told. That theory seemed plausible to me, too: I had no acquaintances in that town; I lived on the far-flung outskirts; to get home, I crossed over railroad tracks, passed by abandoned shacks and through empty lots; in the winter I walked in total darkness. That was an extremely convenient setting for a provocation, for staging an accident, a knife fight, or whatever.

So I decided to return to Aleksandrov literally for a couple of hours, just to show my face to the landlady, to assure her that I hadn't run off. With that done, I would hide out somewhere for a couple of months.

As I am writing this, I wonder what would have happened had I and everyone around me not been so absolutely certain that the authorities would get me for the book. What if I had retained just a grain of hope that I would not be jailed any day? Would I have behaved in the same way? Still, even then, I was making plans for my education and self-education, though I recognized them as "Manilov Projects";* I lacked the self-discipline to proceed with them.

Things might have been different if I hadn't thought my days on the outside were numbered. I might have made an effort to settle in Aleksandrov or some other place near Moscow, to find a better job, get a better place to live.

But what was the point in putting roots down if my days were numbered? So I lived as if at a railroad station; I lived waiting for my train.

Over the ten years that followed I grew accustomed to my life's instability; I started a family, and now, no matter how long we have at a new place, no matter how uncertain our near future, we live as if we will remain there to our dying days, as if we would leave that very nest to our children and grandchildren. We fix up the place to our liking, build our furniture, put a stove together, plant trees, buy books, get the pots and pans. Three times in those ten years we have had to start anew, and, God willing, in a few months, when internal exile ends, we'll start over once again, for the fourth time. We live like the Russian peasants under the khans.

I wonder, could it be that we exaggerated the danger that was hanging over me? We did, perhaps. After all, I wasn't arrested for writing the book; I wasn't even arrested for another seven months.

Reality was not as harsh as we expected.

---

*Manilov is a dreamer in Gogol's *Dead Souls*. (Trans.)

And what if I had stayed clear of social activism, could it have been that I wouldn't have been jailed at all? Or it could have been otherwise: if I had cut my ties to Moscow, then, as a little-known author of an accusatory book, I might have been put away so far that not a trace would have been left.

What's the point in guessing? I was able to draw one practical conclusion from that story: I should not give them a cause for criminal prosecution. Not that this would have guaranteed me freedom, but it would have lowered the risk factor. Unfortunately, it is extremely difficult, if not impossible, to live by this rule. Nearly every Soviet citizen is in violation of some statute, be it passport regulations, statutes against parasitism and vagrancy, or some other administrative rule incorporated into our criminal code. Of course, the militia wouldn't even think of jailing a man who had come to visit his parents and didn't get a residency permit; or an old lady from a village who is living with her children in the city, taking care of a grandson; or people from the countryside near Moscow who regularly spend two days a week with friends in the capital; or those who have residency papers to live in one city but work in another, nearby. But all of these people are in violation of residency rules, and, if necessary, they can be fined, forcibly evicted, or put in the camps. And, in any man's life, the circumstances could become such that it would be easier for him to die than to live in compliance with that law.

In the winter of 1967–68 I didn't even attempt to comply with all those idiotic formalities, thinking that my fate had been sealed anyway.

These days, a certain circle of people has grown accustomed to toptuny stationed by their doorways, to shifts changing under their windows, to being followed on foot and by car. All of it has become a familiar, tiresome part of life. But in late 1967, few had encountered the KGB in interrogations, and, I venture to say, no one lived his daily life under the KGB's sleepless eye. Two notable exceptions were prisoners and those who would be arrested in a matter of days. Still, everyone knew about the informants, the toptuny, the bugging and monitoring of telephones; so, the all-seeing eye and the all-hearing ear seemed to be something mystical and otherworldly, and all the more ominous.

What's more, people still remembered from recent historic experience that contacts with a person honored by the attention of the KGB could be as dangerous as a plague. Just twenty to thirty years earlier that pestilence had wiped out entire apartment buildings, groups of friends, and extended families. So many friendships, so many families had been destroyed by the fear of winding up in the proximity of the infected one.

So what happened in Soviet society in the mid-1960s? Friends had not abandoned the families of the imprisoned Sinyavsky and Daniel; strangers openly offered them help. Every day Daniel got six to ten books or letters from friends, distant acquaintances, and total strangers. Camp censors had their hands full.

In 1967, after *samizdatchiki* Galanskov, Ginzburg, Lashkova, and Doborovolsky were arrested, the same thing happened with their families. I don't recall ever visiting Ginzburg's mother, Ludmilla Ilynichna, and finding her alone. There were always two or three friends of her son who had come to offer help and moral support.

Actually, at one point, Larisa and I went to see her when she was in solitude, though not exactly alone (there was a big crowd). That was in the summer of 1967. Dur-

116

ing the day, we decided to stop by for a visit, so we called to let her know. A neighbor picked up the phone.

"Ludmilla Ilynichna can't come to the phone," she said.

"Is she not well?"

"No, she is well," the neighbor answered with some hesitation.

"She isn't home?"

"No, she's home."

"Is there a search on?" ventured Larisa.

"Yes."

The line went dead.

Without giving it a second thought, we headed for her apartment. On the way, we bought an enormous watermelon, and brought it over.

They let us in, checked our documents, searched Larisa's purse.

"Do you really think people bring samizdat to searches?" she asked.

"How did you find out about the search?" Ludmilla Ilynichna asked.

"We have our own network of agents. So we took all our samizdat, even our A-bomb, and concealed them in a watermelon."

So the gebeshniki had to carve up the watermelon. Then we ate it.

In no more than two days, all our acquaintances had learned from the Little Old Lady—that was Ludmilla Ilynichna's nickname—that Lara and Tolya deliberately showed up at a search. Later we were credited with having started a tradition: as soon as you find out that someone's place is being searched, call up everyone you know, then show up at the search to offer moral support by being there.

. . .

FRIENDS NEVER stopped offering me help and shelter. A young man lent me his student ID; N.P.'s brother and her friend as well as Ira and her friend in effect saved me from encountering the KGB face to face without witnesses.

And once again I marveled at our Moscow intelligentsia, its bravery, its resistance to the actions of the authorities. I, a man obviously followed by the almighty KGB, was being offered places to stay; before the agents' eyes (and their cameras), I was being escorted from place to place, to protect me from their provocations and from encountering them face to face; and no one shunned being seen with me, though I always warned people about the surveillance. I never sought contacts, friendship, or even help; nor could I turn them down. I guess people thought it was their duty to support me. They admired my courage, not noticing their own.

In later years, some of these people dropped out of sight. Others wound up in a circle of people who became increasingly open about their dissent. Still others, either under pressure or on their own, removed themselves from that circle, though I don't think that means that they had changed their views or begun to subscribe to official ideology.

Later, reading Solzhenitsyn's memoirs, I was surprised and disappointed by his reference to a "discovery" he made in 1974: after his arrest and expulsion, there were people who came forth to help his wife and children. The whole thrust of the story is that the authorities had encountered an unforeseen reaction to their crackdown on the writer. In reality, by 1974, the social phenomenon of open resistance and mutual help was at least ten years old. Could Aleksandr Isayevich not have known about it? Could a writer have been unaware of the society's reaction to the Sinyavsky and Daniel trial? Is it possible that he had not given a thought to their case, to its deeper significance? Sinyavsky's and Daniel's names show up in *The Oak and the Calf* as time markers, though their work and their trial made up an entire era in the development of Russian society.

I cannot imagine that Solzhenitsyn doesn't know—or doesn't remember—this. But he hasn't found a place for it in his literary memoir. It reads as if he lived in a desert, where there was only "the oak," the Soviet authorities, and him, the lone and courageous "calf."

After dodging a meeting with an anonymous representative of the KGB (and being followed to Aleksandrov by his spies), I stopped in to see Aunt Nyura, paid the rent for the following two months, and returned to Moscow. I wanted to disappear from their field of vision, and I succeeded. The KGB seemed to have lost me in January and February.

But how long can one remain in hiding?

I stayed with a kind elderly couple, but how long could I burden them with my presence? I came out of "the underground," and a few days later, I was caught in the street and taken to some militia precinct. In an office, I was met by the same man I had met earlier. Now he did not make a secret of who he was.

"I am an official of state security. The name is Semyonov. Please, no questions. I will do the talking. Marchenko, we know everything about you. We know about your book, *My Testimony*, we know that you have sent it abroad and that you are distributing it inside the USSR. There are no plans to prosecute you for it. Please don't take it as a sign of our weakness. Take it as a sign of our humanity. Go back to Aleksandrov, live there and work there like all Soviet people. Nobody needs you!"

Was I dreaming? The KGB showing humanity? This was unheard of. It could not be. They had to have some hidden agenda, but what was it? (I am still racking my brains over it.) Now, more familiar notes started coming through in Semyonov's voice: "Unless you leave Moscow, you will be tried for violation of internal residency regulations. You won't be tried for the book. Live like everyone! Stop throwing mud at the good name of our Motherland! If you don't stop your slander, I am warning you that you will be thrown out of the country."

"To Mordovia. Right?"

"To any country abroad. Didn't you want to escape at some point?" he said sarcastically. Then, evidently adding his own touch to the official warning: "Some hero! You are nothing but a coward. You are hiding from our officials, escaping through the window. All of you scream, 'This is no better than Stalin! This is no better than Stalin!' Let me ask you this. What do you think would be left of you if we were no better than Stalin? Would anyone even bother to talk to you?"

Once again, they demanded that I sign a note promising to leave Moscow, and I left for Aleksandrov.

Who knows, if I had taken Semyonov's warnings and started to "live like everyone," I might have been left alone. I don't know. But I do know that one of Semyonov's predictions indeed came true. I was brought to trial in August 1968. Slandering the state in my writings wasn't the charge; the charge was "violation of passport regulations."

Others stood trial, too. The accusation: reading *My Testimony*.

13

ON AUGUST 21, my trial date, they took me to a barber. A zek has to look respectable before the court and the spectators.

I tried to shave with the razor that the barber, a zek, handed me. I just about howled with pain the instant the blade touched my stubble. I bet that razor had shaved a few dozen like me. I asked for another razor; all I got was a stare, like I'd just asked for a hand grenade.

"Take me back," I said to the guard.

With a look of indifference, he took me back to the holding cell. A bit later they brought in another zek, a young Georgian. He was cut up from shaving, and every now and then he dampened his handkerchief with spit and wiped the blood off his numerous cuts.

My cell mate was a real talker. But he listened as much as he talked—and with equal interest. I told him my story in brief, limiting myself to what was put on record by the prosecution. He was having a hard time grasping what my trial was about; after all, I had a residency permit, even held a job.

"That's fucking nuts," he said. "If you aren't lying through your teeth now, what the hell are they trying you for? You'll walk home straight from the courtroom."

Then he described in detail his "case." He'd been out of the camps for the past six months or so. He'd been doing two or three years for picking pockets and got out at midterm. After getting out, he went back to Georgia, to his mother's. Still, he didn't bother getting a residency permit, just stayed there for a couple of weeks and went off to Moscow. He lived with some woman, not even trying to get a job or a residency permit. He supported himself through professional earnings: sometimes he'd pick a pocket, other times he'd clean out a purse. He got caught in the act once, cleaning out a purse in a store. The militia and the citizens' patrol led him off to the precinct, but he managed to escape on the way. But the case had started; his distinguishing features were put on file. He got caught again, and this time he didn't manage an escape. So now he, too, was about to stand trial, charged with two counts of theft. The fact that he had spent six months without a job or a residency permit wasn't reflected in the charges. It was only mentioned in an evaluation.

So, he predicted, I'd walk from the courtroom.

The article he was tried on could put him in for up to three years, and he said hopefully: "If I get a year, I'll spend the whole day pacing the cell on my hands."

In the courthouse I was allowed a thirty-minute consultation with my attorney, Dina Isaakovna Kaminskaya*; then I was taken to the courtroom. There was a crowd in the hallway. I recognized my friends: Pavel Litvinov, Borya Shragin, Ira, Larisa, N.P., K.B., K.I. Darting between them were those attending for professional reasons, the KGB's toptuny and agents. They didn't come just to have a look at me and listen to the proceedings. They were tailing my friends.

I was led in briskly, but I couldn't help noticing that my friends were unusually agitated. Several of them held

*Defense attorney in a number of dissidents' trials. (Trans.)

newspapers, like they were trying to tell me something. I didn't catch what they were trying to say; I was too tense before the trial.

It was unusual for the whole crowd, "us" and "them," to be allowed into the courtroom. The crime I was accused of was small-time, yet the trial went on from ten in the morning to six at night. I was getting a feeling that it was being stretched out deliberately. And it may have been that their goal was to get the most active people off the streets for the entire day, that day being August 21, 1968.

I didn't know what the problem was. I just felt electricity in the courtroom.

THE SPECTACLE indeed begins theatrically: a small bouquet of flowers is tossed from the courtroom into my hands. Both my militia guards lunge after the bouquet, trying to rip it out of my hands; I don't give it up. I like it. Judge Romanov calls the courtroom—and me—to order, and commands me to hand over the flowers, but I clutch them in my hands, unable to give them away. It is only after seeing anger in Dina Isaakovna's face and realizing that she is not happy with me that I loosen my grip. The guard grabs the bouquet, throws it down, then stomps it into the floor.

I had decided beforehand that I would stay within the limits of the charges brought against me. Talking about actual reasons for the trial would have looked like taking advantage of my reputation. In short, I didn't want to be the one to bring up that subject. Dina Isaakovna approved this stance. After all, an attorney, too, has to steer away from the "irrelevant," even if he grasps a hundred times over just how revelant it is. It would have been unprofessional. And the court would have found it inadmissible. So as it worked out, I had to take part in someone else's game.

Judge Romanov asks idiotic questions about my parents, about their income, and so on. What does that have to do with it? It's just an attempt to create the illusion of an objective proceeding, a smoke screen. I mutter something in response, feeling out of my element, yet playing along with the court.

Prosecutor Zhukov's objective is to demonstrate that I "resided" in Moscow without a residency permit. It's a difficult thing to demonstrate—and difficult to contest. I spent six weeks in a Moscow hospital. Did I "reside" in Moscow during that time, or didn't I? There are hundreds of sick people in that same situation. While I was in the hospital, Larisa, on my request, mailed my rent money to Aunt Nyura, so the prosecution produces the receipt as evidence that I wasn't living in Aleksandrov. That's not anything that needs proving: here's a slip from the hospital.

Working on the book, I spent a few weeks living in a tent in the forest, about a kilometer and a half from Aunt Nyura's. I was at the plant by six every morning, but didn't show up at the "place of residence" daily. Didn't want to waste the time. The prosecutor asserts that during that period I was living in Moscow. "How could I make it from Moscow to the plant every morning? Check the train schedule!" But the court accepts the prosecutor's version.

An Aleksandrov resident can come to Moscow up to three times a week, say, to visit friends or go to the theater; many work in Moscow, as I did for the last few months. Does that mean they "reside" there?

Court discussion of the residency permit law fully reflected its oppressive nature, its applicability to all individuals, as well as its idiocy and the senselessness of its form. After I had a trephination of the skull I asked the militia to give me a temporary permit to stay in Moscow to be under the care of the surgeon who had operated on me. I was refused. It wasn't I who was evading the residency law, it was the militia that had violated it. Still, I am the one who will have to pay the price, because I was the one who "resided."

They had stopped me in the street, checked my documents, and, after determining that I was an out-of-towner, they fined me, threw me out of town, and finally, put me on trial. What is this? Wartime? The time of patrols and police raids? Is Moscow under siege?

After a break, they read the sentence: a year of confinement in a strict-regimen camp. That's the highest penalty provided by law.

As I am led to the voronok, which is parked almost flush against the courthouse door, I once again get a glance at the crowd. Now it has split into two. The agents stand closer to the door, blocking my friends' access to me. Meanwhile, my friends are trying to break through. Two cameras face each other lens to lens; the agents are photographing the crowd, while one of my friends is trying to photograph the agents, or, perhaps, me in the doorway, with the guard detail behind me. Once again I sense an extraordinary tension, the obvious animosity between the two parts of the crowd. They are like two clouds with opposite electrical charges.

My friends were shouting something, but because of my deafness I couldn't make it out. Only after the locked voronok began to move, I heard a fist knocking on its glass and a woman's strong voice: "Tolya, read today's *Pravda!*"

All the way to the Butyrki Prison I wondered, what

could it be, in the newspaper? I made the connection between that shout and my friends' visible agitation. It had to be something serious. But what; not Czechoslovakia? But Dina Isaakovna didn't say anything. (Later I understood: had I known about the invasion, there is no way of knowing what I would have done. My own trial wouldn't have mattered to me, that's for certain.)

In the cell, I tried to find out what had happened, but without asking too many questions. It was senseless to listen in on other conversations, not with the usual noise in the cell. I heard a voice from an upper level of the cell block. "Look here, mate!" I looked up and recognized my acquaintance from the holding cell, the Georgian. He was standing on his head, winking at me.

"What did you get, a year?" I asked, remembering his vow.

He turned over with grace, sat down, and only then answered. "Six months. How about you?"

"A year."

"Like hell you did."

Several other convicts who knew the charges also refused to believe me. "Give it up, stop lying! If they did that, they'd have half the country doing time."

They were right; I wasn't telling the whole truth. But how could I get that day's news? I asked a cell mate sitting next to me, on the floor by the commode.

"Have they given out the newspaper?"

"Sure have."

"Where is it?" I had some guesses about its fate.

"Ripped it up for cigarette papers. What's in there? Amnesty?"

Finally, after asking around, I got the news: Soviet

troops had occupied Prague. I was told about it with complete disinterest; everyone was concerned about his own fate, in no way connecting it with politics. The cell had its own life. At night, some old man got cleaned out. He'd gotten a food parcel that day, eaten some of it, given a little to his immediate neighbors (if you shared with everyone, there wouldn't be a crumb left), and kept what remained: half a pack of sugar and about ten packs of cigarettes. But at night someone cut through his sack and took everything, to the last lump of sugar. The old man took it well, without screams and agitation. Nothing unusual about it: either eat everything at once or keep an eye on your sack.

I had nothing worth guarding. Still, I couldn't sleep that night. I waited for the morning, to get the news on the radio and from the newspaper, which I hoped to get before the others. Were there battles, or did Dubček surrender without a fight? And what if there was the kind of slaughter they had in Hungary in 1956?

At six in the morning, before my cell mates shook themselves out of sleep and began their loud altercations, I moved closer to the radio. What nonsense! "International duty," "fraternal aid," "faithful to the principles . . . ," "the working people of the Soviet Union approve," "all as one!"

I had no doubt that it would happen this way. I knew it for certain, as if I'd sat in on the meetings of the Central Committee. I knew Czechoslovakia would be strangled. But now that it had happened, it was like a boulder had dropped right on top of me. The Czechs weren't treated much differently from us, yet it was a personal insult, a personal humiliation.

What were my friends doing on the outside? What

would I have been doing had I not been locked up here, in prison?

On August 26, I heard about the demonstration of seven people in Red Square.

Pavel, Larisa, Natasha, Kostya, they were all my friends. Delone and I were acquainted. I couldn't recall Dremlyuga and Fainberg; I guess we could have met somewhere, at some gathering. At first I was shaken by the news. Too many people who were dear to me were now in prison, their fate unforeseeable.

What did I think of my friends' action?

I know, there were many opinions on this. Even I was ambivalent at first. Now the authorities were handed the opportunity to put away seven active members of the Resistance. In that sense, the demonstration benefited the authorities. But I also understood that this act of self-sacrifice had been thought through, that it was anything but a lighthearted gesture. Every participant understood that all the roads from Red Square led to prison. But they couldn't live with their country's shame, feeling it as shame of their own. They found just that one way to express their feelings. That demonstration was the sum total of their lives.

Of course, many Russians were appalled by their country's military intervention in a sovereign state. Members of the intelligentsia were more appalled than others, but not everyone had the courage to stand up and protest in the open.

Seven people did.

Later, members of national liberation movements from the Ukraine and the Baltic states told me what they thought about the demonstration. One would think that they, people who had taken up arms to defend their land from the Soviet military machine, would not be awed by a three-minute demonstration in Red Square. But awed they were. They told me: "Yes, we took up arms, but when you do battle, not everyone dies. So everyone has hope, at least a glimmer. Who knows, perhaps I'll be the one who survives. But when you go out protesting in the open, without weapons, just seven of you against the world, well, that takes a special brand of courage."

When my prison train left Moscow, I had yet to hear about the demonstrators' fate. A sense of consternation was never far from me; my friends were on my mind day and night.

From Butyrki, I was sent to the Krasnaya Presnya transit prison. Like the rest of the prisoners, I handed in a postcard with the address of a person who should be notified of where I would be routed. I wrote in N.P.'s address, so she would be able to learn which camp I would be sent to and when. During the three days I spent at Presnya, N.P. managed to get me a food parcel and money, so before my train departed, I was able to spend the ten-ruble allotment at the prison store. It's simply incredible how N.P. always manages to do everything just in time.

What an idiotic situation! I want to say a good word about a good person, yet I dare not mention her name and must hide it behind some initials, as if she is some criminal conspirator. But if I named her, she would have problems at work and get on the KGB watch list. That is, she is on the list as it is (and she's had problems at work), but by openly mentioning her name here, I would in effect be testifying against her. Where else, in what country, could there be a *secret* society devoted to good work and noble deeds? A conspiracy of nonbetrayal? An underground network of aid to children? It's all someone's delirium.

. . .

AT THE railroad station cell at Presnya the word came down that our prison train was going to Kirov, then Perm. "Will they unload us in Kirov, or will they keep going to Perm?" wondered every zek in the Stolypin railroad car.

If we got off in Kirov, that would mean the camp was either in the Kirov oblast or farther north, at Ukhta, in the Komi Autonomous Republic. If they kept going to Perm, there would be no way of telling whether they would leave us in the Perm oblast, with its countless camps along the Urals, or dispatch us farther east. The experienced zeki discussed the pluses and minuses of both alternatives. No matter how they figured it, both came out as the worst possible.

The train was approaching Kirov. (Stations aren't announced on prison trains. The route is kept secret, but zeki know more than your ordinary passengers. They know which camps are closest to the railroad stations, who's the boss at each, and what he is like. They know what the transit prison is like in any given town, and where the prison trains go from there. And what does an ordinary passenger know? Just the bathroom and the railroad station cafeteria.) Names were called out: those were people who had to prepare to exit; they would be staying in Kirov. My name was among them.

In my life as a zek I had passed through Kirov on many a prison train, but I'd never been taken off. This was to be my first encounter with one of the nation's best-known transit prisons. It wouldn't be correct to say that I have been spoiled by the comfort of camps and prisons, yet the Kirov transit prison struck me as one of the worst I had seen. It was filthy, cold, and lice infested.

We were pushed into basement cells, where we stood for three hours straight; there were no benches, just the cement floor. There was watery, sticky dirt underfoot; you wouldn't even have wanted to step in it in your boots.

Here, as in most transit prisons, robbery and face bashing were commonplace. A few convicts had managed to team up and were darting through the crowd in search of loot. They came on to everyone who had a suitcase or a sack. They persuaded others to "give" them their belongings, to "treat" them; threats came next, fights followed. Those difficult to persuade were threatened with razor blades hidden under the sleeves.

Now one of them is milling around me, rubbing up against the half-empty pillowcase I have for luggage, discreetly feeling it with his hands. He's nineteen, no older, but impudent beyond his years.

"Anything in your sack, mate?" he asks. He sounds friendly enough.

"Nothing there that's yours."

"Why the fuck do you scream like you're getting robbed?" Now there is an overtone of threat in his voice. "Just asked you nicely."

"And you were answered nicely. Pipe down."

I do my best to stay calm, to keep my voice low, but I can feel the shakes coming on. He mutters something, then moves on to the other end of the cell, elbowing everyone out of his way. That's where they've gathered, a whole group of them. I know from experience that my encounter with them won't stop here. Soon that guy, accompanied by two others, pushes his way through to me.

"Where are you from, mate?" they ask.

Of course there's nothing special about that question. But I have witnessed many such scenes. This is, shall we say, a prelude. This will be followed with other questions:

131

"What are you in for?" "What did they give you?" and finally, the key question, "What've you got there?" From then on, there are several options, determined by their preferences. If you say that nothing you have is any good, this is followed by the demand "Show us!" or "Let's see!" Some accommodate, and the thieves help themselves to their "gifts" and their "treats." If you don't show them the contents of your sack, one of two things happens: they leave you alone after some threats and a squabble, or they rip the sack out of your hands, take what they want, and graciously return the rest. They could also beat you up and take all there is.

I am familiar with that crowd, so I try to keep my explanations to a minimum: "You aren't interested in me. You're interested in whatever's in my pillowcase. I'll show it to you in the camp, if we wind up in the same one. Unless by that time you have lost interest in other people's sacks."

This time I am fortunate; my plan works. They leave me alone.

As far as I know, such things no longer happen in strict-regimen camps. Robberies and gang terror are a thing of the past. But they are still frequent in camps for first-time offenders, in juvenile colonies, and in transit prisons.

From transit prisons, zeki are taken to camps and prisons around the country, and, chances are, the robber and his victim will never meet again. So the bandit doesn't fear revenge. From this point on, this crowd will no longer brag about its feats. Just the opposite; they will fear being exposed. No matter how impudent, a criminal fears winding up in the same camp with his former victim.

I am taken to another cell, also in the basement. It's

enormous, and it's filled like a barrel of herring. Even its shape is reminiscent of a barrel cut in half lengthwise. The cots are up against both walls and in two rows down the middle. The passageways are taken up with wooden platforms, with zeki sleeping on them. The ceiling is curved, so if your cot is on the edge, you can barely stuff your legs between the bed and the ceiling. The tiny opening, which only symbolically can be called a window, is down in a hole, below ground level. There's a grid on top of the hole, too. The tobacco, the sweat, the breath, and the latrine pail in the corner make the air thick, heavy, and sticky, like the floor by the latrine pail. The prison must be saving a bundle on fuel: even in winter, even without heat, the cells are hot and stuffy, and the zeki are down to their underwear, sweaty from head to toe.

At the end of the hall is a small lavatory, filthy in the extreme. We are taken there twice a day. Not everyone from the cell fits in, so the guards stuff us in, like into a voronok, pushing the last one in with the door. After a big to-do, they start taking us there half a cell at a time, accordingly cutting the time allotment in half. Each time we are taken there, fights flare up in the cell; nobody wants to carry out the latrine pail. Sometimes the guards, having had it with the constant battles over the latrine pail, let it sit till the next time. Then the contents pour over the sides. The zeki cuss, but once again, there is the same battle over who is to carry the pail.

These days latrine pails have been removed from most prisons. Our civilization has reached the level where the rusted bucket from the era of Catherine the Great has been replaced with a commode in a corner of the cell. Though it usually leaks, and though there is little that is appealing about one hundred people satisfying their needs in the same place where they eat and sleep, the commode still is a great blessing, a colossal step in mankind's march down the road of progress. That achievement took at least as much time and effort as the exploration of space.

In Kirov I, too, got cleaned out, just like the old man in Butyrki. I didn't have much, only the remnants of the parcel and what I'd gotten at the prison store. Just like the old man, in the evening I treated my immediate neighbors, and at night found my sack empty. When you get robbed, you feel ashamed, humiliated. And then there's anger. You don't know who did it, yet you have to deal with the people around you, including those who cleaned you out. There are decent people around you, but try to distinguish them from the others when you're acquainted for a day or two, and then it's farewell.

In the worst case, I expected to be sent to the extreme north from Kirov. Instead, I was sent on to Perm. So what was the point of getting me off the prison train that was going there anyhow and marinating me in this half-barrel?

After Perm, I was put on another prison train, and by mid-November, I reached Solikamsk. It took two months to travel 2,000 kilometers, which averages out to 30 to 35 kilometers a day. It would have been three or four times as fast to do that trip in a horse cart, with gendarmes. Even on foot I could have made it in the same time!

This was the end of the trip, thank God. There's just one way from Solikamsk—to the camps.

But in Solikamsk I was held back for another month and a half. They didn't ship me out right away because it was too late. They had to wait for the Ural rivers to freeze over. In the spring and fall, forest camps on the Krasnyy Bereg at Nyrob are inaccessible.

Actually, in accordance with my medical evaluation ("fit for labor; exceptions: heights and lumbering"), I should have been kept in Solikamsk itself. There is a strict-regimen camp here, just behind the transit prison. The work here is construction; in the woods, everyone knows, it's tree felling. The conditions in Solikamsk are better; so are the rations. That being the case, it's not for me.

The Solikamsk prison was filthy and crowded, no better than in Kirov. Still, the wait was somehow easier. It was the end of the road, and that counted for something. On top of that, zeki behaved differently there. Nobody knew if he'd wind up in the same camp with his bunk mate, so everyone had to be treated with tolerance, without impudence.

Despite prison rules, there was no reveille, no taps here. Card games went on around the clock. Players hardly bothered to conceal their gambling from the guards. At night they took their cards to upper bunks, closer to the feeble light bulb in the niche by the cell door.

They played for everything: old rags, food, new clothes, money. Here you could observe the wild swings of fortune. A zek could get in the game with nothing but a pair of worn socks and a washed-out handkerchief to his name, then, in a matter of hours, his holdings would increase to a huge pile of threads, food, and money. Or you could observe a snazzy dresser in a silk shirt and a good suit with a sackful of goods. He would turn his nose up at prison slop and order the forbidden tea, *anasha* grass, even morphine, not to mention food, from the guards. A day later he would sit on a bare bunk, in worn-out camp-issue pants, a pea coat, and socks that had gone through thirty-three terms and in which seven men had been buried.

Of all the hard-core cardplayers, I remember Zhora best. By the time I got to the cell, he was wearing pitiful rags. A few times he tried to get back on the winning streak, though I don't know what he could offer his partners. Luck wasn't with him. After every loss, he would spend about three hours in silence, lying facedown on the bunk; then he would come square out in the center of the cell, lean his shoulder against the pillar, and quietly sing old Russian romances. He had a pleasant voice, and he sang with abandon, tuning out everything around him. When he sang, the cell became uncharacteristically quiet; even the card games stopped. Any zek who interrupted was told to shut up.

Zhora sang only when he was moved to. He never took requests. He didn't wait for things to quiet down, and sometimes started right in the midst of the prison din. Once, after losing again, he started making his way to the upper bunk to cope with his loss in silence.

"So, Zhorik, why not sing to us now?" someone said derisively.

"In this mood, singing's the last thing . . . ," he said, dropping facedown on the beat-up pea coat he used for a pillow.

There was another cardplayer, a typical one. He was well dressed and looked down on everyone. Other players asked him to mediate arguments. And he kept up his high standing by telling stories about that time in a card game when he banged someone's eye out, broke someone's arm, and chased someone else under a bunk. All that in the name of fairness and the law of cards.

Three days or so after my arrival, another party of convicts was brought in from Perm. In the evening that dandy talked some new guy into staying up and playing cards. The game went through the night, and ended in a morning fistfight. I don't know if the new guy had won "fairly" or if he had cheated along the way. The two started arguing, each trying to prove his side. Generally, in such cases cardplayers call in a third party to judge who is right. But those two didn't turn to anyone, and their run-in was getting louder and more insulting. In the end, the new guy, with a swift kick, pushed the dandy from the bunk to the floor. It was a cement floor, and he dropped from the upper bunk. He was hurt so badly that he couldn't get up right away. He hid himself away on the lower bunk, and for several days didn't even come out to the latrine. It was the end of that argument.

The new guy wasn't a king for long. The next day he lost everything, to the last thread. And by the time I was being shipped out, their souls were in harmony, though both had become the cell flops, inconsequential, penniless paupers.

Commerce burgeons alongside gambling in transit prisons. Zeki try to sell all they've got to the staff; you can't wear your own clothes in the camps, and state-issued clothes are not something worth holding onto. The trusties on the prison staff, working with the guards, bring in the forbidden tea, anasha grass, vodka. The prices are determined by degree of scarcity. Once I saw a cell mate trade a new overcoat (worth ninety to one hundred rubles) for seven packs of tea. A relatively new, decent suit brought four to five packs; a pair of pants or a shirt went for just one pack. Incidentally, in a store just outside prison gates, a pack of tea sells for thirty-eight to forty-eight kopeks. Not a bad profit for the guards and the staff!

I didn't gamble, didn't trade, so what was there for me to do in the cell? I didn't have any writing paper, and neither did any of my cell mates. There wasn't a book in sight; there are no libraries in transit. I was so bored, I could just have reached for the cards!

I sent a letter to Moscow, just in case, and to make sure that it got there, I signed it with the first name that came to mind. There was some chance that in the disarray of transit prisons they wouldn't be able to tell who'd sent it. Sure enough, about two weeks later I got several letters and packages at once. (The first letters and telegrams got to Perm before I did.) The packages contained books, paper, ballpoint pens (right there, in the censor's office, a trusty offered me two packs of tea for the pens, but I needed the pens, not the tea); each package contained a chocolate bar. That's forbidden, but the complacent censor, after grumbling some, let me keep it. And there was soap, wrapped in an old issue of *Vechernyaya Moskva*. I realized immediately that the paper was there for a reason.

LATER THAT EVENING, I settled down to hot water and chocolate. The books were passed around the cell, and I looked through *Vechorka*. Just as I thought, here was the news item about the trial of the Red Square demonstrators. Larisa, Pavel, and Kostya got internal exile; Dremlyuga and Delone got the camps. That bit of news calmed me down a bit. At least three of them didn't get the camps. But even internal is no picnic; and that's to say nothing of the trip there, especially if it's on prison trains! I was especially worried about Larisa. How would she handle the prison trains? Which place would she "luck into"? She was the only woman convicted. At that time I didn't even suspect that Natasha Gorbanevskaya would have to spend several years in a psychiatric hospital.

I didn't worry so much about the men. It's good to

feel on your own hide all the hardships of a convict's life. The fortitude of the spirit, too, is better tested here.

Now I had something to do in my cell. I read and reread the books that had been sent to me, though they were really nothing. (That's what I'd asked for in the letter: just as long as it's in print, no need to have good books perish.) I had other work, too.

Back in Perm, I had been given a telegram from L.Z. YOU CAN AND MUST BECOME A REAL PROFESSIONAL WRITER, it said. What L.Z. meant was that I needed self-education, professional training. Where I was, that seemed impossible; I had no book list, no books, no idea of how to proceed. But I did have an abundance of free time. I didn't have this much time on the outside, and I wouldn't have it in the camp. So I started to think up and develop plans for a novel, then another one, then a third. The plots intertwined, then diverged; they filled out with detail; the heroes I had created were acquiring biographies, their features were changing as they adjusted to each other and to their lives. Every day I could watch each story as in a film, or I could watch clips from all three. It was terribly interesting to follow a hero through situations, with me knowing his fate and him unaware of it. But I began to get confused, to run into problems and inconsistencies. I had to write something down—even if it was in code, even if it was just an outline.

In Perm, I managed to put together brief, schematic outlines of two novels and record them in coded phrases. But, during a surprise search, my notebooks disappeared. I went looking for them—but no results. "What notebooks? Vanished? Who needs them, who needs your paper soilings?" was the answer I got from the deputy prison chief. I had to accept the loss.

No use crying. In Solikamsk, after getting pens and paper, I started anew. I filled a few notebooks, once again using coded phrases. Nothing there even resembled "criminal content." Still, I knew that the notebooks would be taken away in the next search, and I tried to develop an even more ingenious code. On top of that, just in case, I memorized everything.

I watched my mental movies through late December, until the rivers froze up and we were gathered to be shipped to Nyrob.

14

Ours was a large party, about 150 men getting shipped to strict- and special-regimen camps. We would be taken by truck, and the trip would be seven hours or so on a firm winter road. It doesn't take long to get frostbitten in the Northern Urals in December, so we were ordered to put on all the clothes we had, from warm underwear to cotton-stuffed work jackets, with pea coats on top. Every zek turned into a thick, unwieldy, cotton-stuffed doll. The guards were wearing sheepskin jackets under sheepskin coats so enormous that they dragged behind them. They, too, looked like dolls, just of a different silhouette.

There were forty zeki to a truck, a huge three-axle Ural with high boards and the front part of the bed walled off for three or four guards and a dog. It seemed there would be no way we'd get in, but the guards were experienced. They led us into the truck bed, six in a row.

"Attention! Everyone raise arms, I will count to three. On three everyone's to sit down not lowering the arms." And, indeed, with our arms up, we more or less managed to sit down on the floor. Bringing our arms down was now a problem. We started to shift and wiggle, trying to squeeze our arms back down one way or another. That was of no concern to the guards. We sat with our backs to them, and we were forbidden to turn around or hold onto the sides of the truck.

The road from Solikamsk to Nyrob goes through the

taiga. It was blanketed in snow, especially the pines. Every time the trucks reached the top of the *sopki,* you could see great expanses, the taiga, and more taiga.

On the way we passed through Cherdyn. With great interest I looked at the famous settlement. Here the Mandelstams spent their internal exile; I had just read Nadezhda Yakovlevna's memoirs in Moscow. Who would have known about this Cherdyn if not for Osip Emilye-vich? Feeble houses, the taiga all around! But now and again a brick house happened by, and you couldn't get enough looking at it. They were old houses, made of choice red brick, and even the outbuildings were brick. Wealthy hunters and lumber merchants must have lived here before the Revolution.

The same brick went into an attractive, but uncared-for, crumbling church. Cherdyn stands on the Vishera River. We crossed it over the ice.

WE REACHED Nyrob by dusk. In the winter, nights come early here. There were two zones, strict and special regimen. While we were waiting to be let in, two columns of zeki passed by, wearing stripes. Everything was striped, the pea coats, work jackets, pants, hats.

The special-regimen camp prepared wood for sending downstream. Those prisoners weren't used in lumbering or on the rafts, for fear of escapes.

After a search, we were taken along the perimeter of the zone to a fenced-off barrack. This was the inner-camp prison and the transit office. Here they processed the "distant taiga business trips." But in the morning I found out that I would not be sent into the taiga; I would remain here, in Nyrob itself. I would live in what one may call the capital! The others envied me.

. . .

"WHAT? You've been sent here with such a term!" The camp warden is puzzled. He has called me in "to get acquainted."

"They didn't ask me."

"A year's term, and by the time he gets here, seven months is all that's left!" The warden looks through my papers and stumbles across my medical evaluation, with its limitations on labor.

"And why do they keep sending his kind here! I need mules, all I've got is lumber. What will I do with you?"

I remain silent. An officer comes up to the camp warden, leans low over the desk, and whispers something straight into the warden's ear. The warden listens attentively, looking up at me with curiosity.

From then on he asked no questions.

That day I made another acquaintance, the KGB officer, Senior Lieutenant Antonov. When the KGB officer calls, you go, no sense in refusing. The conversation was unpleasant. It was threatening, and it dragged on. "Don't even think that you'll just do your time and go, Marchenko. There's time for you, and more time; you'll rot in the camps. You won't get away from me, not till you learn to think straight. This isn't Moscow, remember that," and so on.

"Just tell me straight, what do you want of me?" I asked.

"I'm telling you straight. Don't you get it? Well, think, think while there's time. And when you are done thinking, come right here. We'll write it together."

"I've already written what I wanted to write, without your help."

"Mark my words, Marchenko, you'll regret this."

You could say I had received a "fair warning." But where would they strike from? And when?

The conversation left a bad taste in my mouth.

Anything can happen in a camp. Two zeki can get in a fight, and one can knife the other in the back. Or the guards can shoot you during an "escape attempt." A brick can fall on your head. Or they can torch an outhouse and accuse you of attempting to burn down the zone. You have to walk around looking over your shoulder, waiting for the provocation that could come any minute. It doesn't take much of this to drive you crazy. So I cleared my mind of those thoughts.

Even without all that, my situation in the camp wasn't simple. I was put in a construction brigade. That work was easier, more agreeable work than the camp's specialty, lumbering. The "woodsmen" were trucked from the camps to the lumbering sites, about an hour and a half each way, plus the search, plus the wait, and there were times when the trucks broke down. When that happens, you sit in the open truck bed, in the frost, waiting for them to fix the truck or bring in another one. Our "woodsmen" had been known to return to the zone at three or four in the morning. They'd be back at work at seven.

Our brigade, the fourteen of us, worked in the settlement, about five minutes' walk from the residential zone. That alone was a great stroke of luck. It was the place the exemplary "woodsmen" were transferred "to rest up" after a few years of hard work and no problems. The exemplary stoolies and ass lickers worked there, too. And there I was, transferred straight on arrival. That was hard to understand, and it was suspicious, so the brigade members tried to feel me out, to see for what merit—or for what reason—I'd landed in their brigade.

But before I got too comfortable, I was shifted to another brigade; it, too, did construction, and there were no long trips to work. But these men earned their breaks differently. They were all long-termers, the heavyweights, doing ten to fifteen years, the maximum, "exceptional" penalties. They were former death-row convicts who got their sentences commuted to camp or prison. They were in for especially dangerous crimes: the more heinous rapes, murders, robberies. Most men in the brigade were transferred after doing half their terms at the special-regimen camp, so when our column passed a column of the "striped ones," news and greetings went both ways, despite shouts from the guards. That brigade didn't work in the woods because most long-termers are believed—correctly—to be likely to escape. It was because of them that the work zone was fenced off with a 2-meter wooden fence and two rows of barbed wire and guarded by a beefed-up detail, which included a machine gunner on every guard tower. In addition to the usual head count before work and after, the brigade was counted up, then recounted and checked against index cards. And if the head of the guard detail suspected that someone was missing, the whole brigade was lined up, broken up into groups of five, then checked against index cards.

So there I was, doing a year for some piddling violation of passport rules, lumped in with the heavyweights. What's more, I was transferred along with the cook from my first brigade, Herman Andreyev, a provocateur famous throughout the camp and outside it for being a "staff witness" in all criminal cases that originated in the camp. He was a drug addict, and thus under the total control of the administration. Of course, the men in the brigade decided immediately that the two of us were sent in as informers for the administration and the KGB. They should have thought a bit harder. What good is a deaf informer? And what's the use of sending in a new informer when there are enough of them in the brigade as it is? On second thought, the KGB has been known to do such things to test their informers. As they say, you need a spy for every spy. I, too, had some suspicions about Herman. He had to have been transferred with me for a reason. Those suspicions were confirmed in the end. But more on that later.

I decided to keep my ideas and explanations to myself. Besides, no one was saying anything to my face. So I didn't tell anyone anything about myself, except what my sentence was. Explanations would lead nowhere, and excessive frankness is simply dangerous. To avoid getting drawn into the usual zek banter, I took books, newspapers, and notebooks to work. (Actually, that's not allowed, and if anything of the sort is found in a search, it's confiscated. "It's not the library you're going to!" But a zek can bring anything through, if he has to.)

Reading time was in abundance. We were taken to work in the mornings, when the temperature was less than 50 below. We rushed to the construction site, and as soon as the gates were opened, ran as fast as we could to the shelter. We made a fire and for the following hour and a half stayed as close as we could to the stove, trying to keep warm. When the place warmed up, we spread out to while away the hours. The administration looked the other way. All that mattered was that the day was counted, that the brigade had been brought out to work. The work quota could be squeezed out of a zek on warmer days.

So there I sat, reading in my lawful place in the shelter. Cardplayers gathered in the other corner. Here, as in transit, they gambled for everything: clothes, parcels from relatives, future store allotments. Some busied themselves with strategies for getting free men to bring in vodka, moonshine, or cologne.

Naturally, money was prohibited in the camps, although it was around. It could be obtained through a simple mail operation: a zek transferred his earnings to relatives and simultaneously, in secret, gave them the name of a local resident with whom he had already made the necessary arrangements. The relatives sent the money back to Nyrob, to the specified address, and the local either passed the money over to the zek or filled his order. Of course, there was a commission involved.

I, too, could have made use of this well-tested method, but I figured camp rations were enough for what little time remained of my term.

In political camps such operations were almost unthinkable. The administration was more vigilant, seeing to it that the zek was cut off from the outside. Camps for common criminals weren't so strict, and it could well have been that the administration knew about those channels and was either skimming commissions or controlling the whole trade, to keep the reins in its hands.

Money could buy anything—food, alcohol, drugs, even a release from work. Pay the brigade fifteen rubles or so, cash, and you don't have to work for a month. The brigade leader will mark you as "present," and the brigade will fill your quota.

15

ZEKI HAD another diversion—women.

I hear people say, "The camps don't interest me. I've been there, I've seen it all, there's nothing new." Not so. There is something new every term. In Nyrob, for the first time, I encountered covert prostitution in the camps. I'd heard about it before, but refused to believe it. Here the world's oldest profession was practiced by women who had been sent out of Moscow and Leningrad for "parasitism."

Demand for women is high among prisoners and soldiers. Still, I cannot report that the trade made our women wealthy. Everyone paid what he could. Sometimes it was money, sometimes threads, sometimes a scoop of camp porridge. So the women did it for the love of their art and, as they say, in order to protect their professional standing.

A few of these "parasites" served the officers and the administration. They lived well, were unavailable to soldiers and convicts, and looked down on their less fortunate colleagues. The officers' wives hated them with a passion, and were known to cuss them out in public, in the streets of the settlement. The "parasites" never yielded the last word, and their vocabulary was richer than that of the lawful wives. For a column of zeki led to work, such scenes were a substitute for theater.

But how did the "parasites" work the inmates, who, after all, were cordoned off by fences, guard towers, and soldiers with machine guns?

Construction and lumbering sites were guarded only during work time. After work, the guards left. So, during work time, zeki built a hideout, a bunker, and, through camp mail, let the "parasites" know about it. At night, the ladies freely entered the work zone, moved into the bunker, and lived there for a month or more, not seeing the light of day, even when nature called. The bunkers were equipped with piss buckets, which zeki emptied out.

Generally the "parasites" worked in groups of three or four, serving the same brigade. Every work area had its own bunker. The ladies respected one another's "spheres of influence." Whenever encroachments occurred, they were classified as "betrayal" and were followed by turbulent arguments and battles.

The making of a bunker took some effort and creativity. Bunks were knocked together for the inside, and the outside was thoroughly camouflaged. To throw the guard dogs off scent, the place was sprinkled with homegrown tobacco, chlorine, gasoline, and so on.

Our strictly guarded brigade also had its bordello. For the first few days, before the others got to know me, they tried to hide its existence from me. They managed, at first. Nothing in their lives was of interest to me. Besides, they knew that my hearing was poor, so that facet of the life of our collective was generally discussed in hushed voices so I wouldn't overhear. But you cannot hide an awl in a sack. You can't hide a live person, either. At first I guessed about it all, then I saw it for myself.

Our shelter had two rooms. In the larger of the two, under the floor, the zeki had built a third, and that was where a "parasite" lived. At times, whenever there was an infusion of cash into the brigade, she shared those quarters with others.

Our "parasites" had a better deal than the ones in the forest. At night they could walk out to get some fresh air, or simply climb out from underground and spend some time in a room. We even hosted a guest appearance by two "parasites" from Cherdyn.

Our brigade was building a garage. The walls and the ceiling were already up, and we were digging holes in the floor, beneath where the cars would be. The brigade decided to build a permanent bunker-bordello as well. So, next to a hole under one of the parking slots, we dug another big hole. The roof was concrete and the entrance was through a niche for mechanics' tools. One side of the niche, a concrete panel, was mounted on hinges. It was a heavy door, which closed tightly from the inside. It would have taken explosives to open it from the outside.

The new bunker was more spacious than the old one. It had real bunks, accommodations for four, a table, even a couple of benches. We dragged in an electric cable and set up heat and lighting. There was also an electric hot plate.

The bunker was constructed with my direct participation, and it became "operational" before I left.

Our bordello could not be found, not even with dogs. Though our brigade had its share of stoolies, nobody ever gave away the hideout and the women: the men's natural need for women overwhelmed other basic drives. The administration sensed there were women in the zone, but no matter how hard they searched, none were found.

There were a few interesting methods of paying for

services. When someone in the brigade had money, the ladies got a ruble per visit. Then only the person with the ruble had access to them.

But when zeki had nothing, the "parasites" found themselves in dire straits. There was nothing for them outside, no money, nothing to eat. Here, at least, they could get a scoop of our slop or porridge. And since our food came from a shared pot, at feeding time anyone was able to descend to the bunker. Once I saw two pals go in carrying a pair of worn socks, one sock per guy. That turned out to be enough.

The women were never sober. There was always something to drink in the bunker, be it vodka, samogon, home brew, cologne, brake fluid.

Our priestesses of love were drunk, filthy, dressed in pitiful rags, and so tattered that you couldn't tell their age. (Actually, the age spread is significant, from nineteen or twenty to fifty and up, "from Young Pioneers to pensioners.") They were so unattractive that there were times when a zek descended into the bunker, then came back up shaking his head. "No, just can't, nothing happens."

Still, it wasn't just the zeki, but the guards, too, who had claims to their ministrations. The "parasites," in apparent solidarity with the zeki, virulently hated the guards, and worked them only through the convicts' mediation.

Once I observed this scene: the entire brigade was talking a "parasite" into "giving" to a soldier. She had just thrown him out of her bunker, and he returned to the brigade to complain. She was unmoved by their arguments, and it was only the fear of being turned in by the dejected soldier that finally broke her pride. I also knew of two soldiers from our guard detachment who were visiting our old bunker in secret from each other and everyone else.

Our "parasites" were also known to climb out of the bunker and spend time among the zeki. In the winter they would be wearing the same clothes as the men. Cotton-stuffed pants, pea coats, and hats made them indistinguishable from us. So many discussions were taking place in front of me, in the shelter.

I guess there are people who would read these pages with repugnance. "Criminals. What else do you expect?" But let me quote a passage about politicals: "In the evening a girl was put in an empty barrel, a guard opened the prison doors, the girl was let out, and another guard led her into the convicts' rooms. The next morning, the same way was used to get the girl out of the prison.... The same caper succeeded a few times thereafter.... There was so much gratitude from the convicts!"

Those convicts weren't common criminals. They were the Decembrists. It was Polina Annenkova, the wife of a Decembrist, who arranged for them to break the fast. She hired a girl, bribed the water man and the guards. She didn't do it with contempt and repugnance, but with understanding of human nature. M. M. Popov, a gendarme, gives a similar account of this episode: "Most convicts of the Petrov prison were single; they were young men, their blood hot and in need of women. The wives devoted much time to finding ways to resolve this grievous problem."*

OUR "PARASITES" were fallen creatures. In my view, they were no longer human.

---

*The Memoirs of Polina Annenkova (Krasnoyarsk, 1977), p. 291.

It is up to sociologists, psychologists, and physicians to pinpoint the cause of this problem. I am not about to blame our political system for the existence of these fallen people. I'll leave it to Marxist sociologists to explain everything through political and economic causes which lead them to conclude that the "underclass" is the product of capitalism and that no such stratum exists in our country.

Like hell it doesn't! Remote towns and villages are full of "parasites," male and female, exiled and homegrown. They have no shelter, they have no family, and they never will have, either. They aren't looking for them. They don't need them. They have no possessions; all they have is on their backs. They have but one goal: to find something to drink, to numb themselves. In Chuna they aren't hard to find. They gather in an empty lot by the store; they lie here, drunk, men and women, young and old, locals and exiles, sprawled on top of a layer of broken glass. After sleeping it off, still wobbly, they drift toward the store, hoping to get something else to drink. That's all they care about. And no one here cares about them.

In the capitals and towns visited by foreigners such people are virtually nonexistent. The militia throws them out, using passport regulations and vagrancy and parasitism statutes. So all sorts of visiting celebrities—for instance, Muhammad Ali—tell the world: "I was amazed to meet no paupers and no prostitutes in the USSR." If Muhammad Ali never met them, it means they really don't exist. (The same applies to agents of state security, whom he hadn't "met" either. They met him, all right; they saw him off, too.) What is the point of our propaganda? Do they really think I would believe a guest before I'd believe my own eyes?

But let's not worry about Muhammad Ali; he doesn't

care about our country, all he did was pop in and pop out. It's far more alarming that our press, our scientists, and our authorities deliberately look away from the hemorrhages of our society; we don't study them, we don't treat them; all we do is hide them under the robes of festivals and olympiads. But sniff the air: stench drifts out from under those robes.

16

THE WINTER of 1968–69 was a cold one. In Nyrob, it was 56 or 57 below every morning. Larisa wrote to me that where she was, days always began at 58 below. The letter was from the town of Chuna, in the Irkutsk oblast. Chuna? Sounds like *chuma*.* My camp acquaintances offered some descriptions: it was a cursed place, a chuma indeed.

THESE DAYS you cannot see any camps in Chuna, in its vicinity, or anyplace along the Tayshet-Bratsk Road. But in 1971, I had to take a small airplane from Bratsk to Chuna, and from above I could see the clearly marked square "zones" with guard towers on every corner. They are kept out of sight.

About ten minutes' walk from Chuna, one can still find abandoned narrow roads that zeki cut through the taiga. Chuna itself has a number of monuments of camp architecture: a club built using a standard camp blueprint (I have seen identical ones in Karaganda, in the Urals, in Mordovia); a bathhouse with a date laid out in brick on the facade, "1957." Old camp barracks are still around, too, though more and more of them are being demolished. For some reason they aren't being preserved for future generations as historic monuments. There are lots

---

*The plague. (Trans.)

of "Westerners" here, Ukrainians, Lithuanians, Russians, all of them former zeki. This stretch of the Baikal-Amur Highway, "the highway of the century," was built by Russian zeki and Japanese prisoners of war.

WE DIDN'T WORK much in those frosts; still, it was enough. When we returned to the residential zone, I was wet and covered with mud. And since they didn't issue me a work jacket, I had nothing to change to.

"You'll get it when the next party of prisoners comes in," I was told. So I waited. I waited for a month and a half, but no work jacket. My requests, and the requests of the brigade chief, were simply ignored by the head of the work unit.

Finally, I said, "I don't work until I get my jacket."

"You'll work," he said. "Either that or I put you in a punishment cell."

The following day I stopped work. I would go out to the site with the others, then either sit in the shelter or, on milder days, make a path for myself and walk around. The brigade chief didn't try to get me out to work. He knew that was my way of standing up for my rights. I was certain that he was putting "no-shows" on my work sheet. I waited for the bosses to react. Then, all of a sudden, I found out that the brigade chief was continuing to mark off workdays. That meant that at the end of the month I would get the same pay as the others in the brigade. I'd be taking money from those who'd worked.

So I had to have a chat with the brigade chief.

"Mark me absent. I'm not at work."

"I can't. I've never helped anyone get into the punishment cell."

Dvoretsky was different from other zek brigade chiefs. He was put in that place because of his background in construction, and he saw his position as a burden. He shied away from forcing convicts to work and didn't try to please the bosses. (He didn't last long as the brigade chief. Before I left, he was replaced by someone more appropriate, Sapozhnikov.)

"You aren't the one who'll be throwing me in a punishment cell," I said. "The head of the work unit will."

"I am not his helper. I am a zek, like you are. I'm a big shot today; tomorrow you and I will be carrying the same stretcher."

There is an unwritten zek rule: if you don't want to work, stay in the residential zone, don't go out on site. Then it's the administration that puts you in a punishment cell, and the brigade chief doesn't lose face before fellow convicts. I didn't want to give them a legal cause for the punishment. I came out to the site because I was "seasonally dressed." I had the pants, the vest, and a hat, which had been issued to me in Solikamsk. But without the work jacket I had a right not to work. So, with Dvoretsky's help or without, there would be someone who would report my "sabotage" to the administration.

Sure enough, a couple of days later, the head of the work unit stopped over at our shelter. He got the brigade together and started his work-over:

"Don't want to work, eh? Dodging? You, Marchenko, are a malicious violator of the regimen!"

"No, you are the one in violation of the regimen. You haven't given me a work jacket. It's been two months!"

"Well, then, I'll put you in a punishment cell for insults. We got ourselves an intellectual here, get his work jacket ready."

A day passed, then another, and another. The head of the work unit had yet to make good on his threat. He did start to set the brigade members against me, saying that I was ripping them off by not working. When I took him on in front of everyone, I had the sympathy of other convicts. They could see that I was demanding what was mine, that I was making no secret of refusing to work, and that I was not hiding behind their backs. Generally, in any altercation with the bosses, zeki back their own. But after some reinterpretation of the events, a few of them started casting unfriendly glances toward me, even threatening to "take care" of me. "The bosses won't come to defend you." Once, a zek lunged at me with a hammer. I raised a shovel. The situation was not resolved; others broke it up.

It was only two weeks later that the head of the work unit finally threw me in a punishment cell for seven days. His order read that I was "dressed fully," but after the punishment cell they gave me a work jacket. So what, if I may ask, was the reason for punishment? But whom do you ask?

MEANWHILE, winter was waning, and my term with it. I hadn't had any run-ins, or, for that matter, encounters, with the KGB officer Antonov. Nonetheless, his threat hung over me like an ax. I had a few minor run-ins with a major in charge of the Cultural-Educational Department, after I received two book parcels that he refused to give me.

"You've been sent here to serve a term, not to read books. Isn't the camp library enough for you?"

"It isn't."

"Books from the outside will not be delivered."

"Why not?"

"Why not? Why not? You're all too literate these days. You all know your rights. If something's not to your liking, all I hear's 'Why, for what reason, on whose authority?' "

"Still, why can't I receive books from the outside?"

"I know how you read in the camps. You get your fill of Flaubert, then jerk off all night."

I wanted to ask the cultural-educational officer whether he was familiar with that writer and whether he had experienced his power personally. But I didn't want to do battle on unfamiliar terrain: I had not read Flaubert. So I asked about something else.

"Is Lenin approved for reading in the camps?"

The major paused, then answered calmly, "Lenin. We'll think about it."

In the end he let me keep the parcels, apparently because they contained books that, in his judgment, were safer than Flaubert.

That spring I once again wound up in the punishment cell. The reason this time was analogous to the first: I refused to work. This time I didn't come out to the work zone. We were pouring tar on the roof of the garage, and we had to carry stretchers 5 meters up a narrow, slick ramp without handrails. Healthy guys had been known to fall off that ramp, and I am prone to dizzy spells. When I told the head of the work unit, he sneered. "You call that height? It's not space we are launching you into!" He refused to shift me to another job.

After I finally fell off the ramp, together with that stretcher, I decided that spending the rest of my term in a punishment cell, even on a penalty ration, would be better than getting crippled. By that time I had only two and a half months to go.

On May 20, I finished my fifteen days in the cell. If I didn't come out to work, I'd be put in the cell again. But at least in the meantime I'd manage to wash up with soap (in Nyrob's punishment cells they took away your soap and toothbrush: "It's not a sanatorium!") and pick up the letters that had piled up over two weeks.

To my surprise, I wasn't allowed into the zone. I would be sent to another camp, I was told.

Now that's something! A new camp two months before the end of the term. It just doesn't bode well, I thought. I wasn't even allowed to pack up; someone at the barrack tied up my sack and brought it to me at the inner-camp prison. I looked through it, not finding the most important of my possessions, my notebooks. I'd had four of them, but one was all I got back. That one had the notes I'd made while reading Herzen, Korolenko, Uspensky, and others. The three that contained my own notes and the outlines of future novels that I'd reconstructed after the search in Perm had once again fallen into the hands of the chief arbiters of literature.

They wouldn't be able to boil porridge out of those notes. It was all code: "at a search ... the queen of spades." What could they get out of that? Not a thing. Still, I would no longer have those notebooks, and for them that was an accomplishment—and a certain pleasure.

Much later, on the outside, during searches, I lost everything I managed to write—the outlines, the rough drafts. Could it be that all of it is kept someplace in the KGB archives, under *M*? No, it must have been burned in the special crematorium for manuscripts, after being classified as "materials that could be used for writing anti-Soviet works." That was the exact reason given to me for a confiscation in 1974. Who are those experts? Professors of literature? Who gave them their doctorates? Or are they just ordinary scholars in plain clothes? I'd love to find out.

Later Vladimir Maksimov chided me for not working in a manner befitting a Soviet writer: write several copies at once, he told me. Then, immediately, hide the copies in different places. That's how he, Maksimov, operates. So some copies get confiscated, but at least one survives.

Could that have been just what L.Z. meant in his telegram, "You can and must become a real professional writer"? That is, as Solzhenitsyn wrote, a writer-conspirator. I'm learning. I am.

To be honest, learning that is a bit easier than learning to write.

17

FOUR OTHER zeki and I were loaded into a truck and sent to Valay, the worst of the Nyrob camps.

The isolated taiga settlement and the small camp where we were taken had a depressing look about them. The shabby, rotten houses in the settlement and the barracks in the camp had settled into the ground up to the windows. Whenever someone passed by the barrack window, all you could see was feet. It seemed that if a strong wind blew and pushed over a house on the edge, the others would topple like dominoes. And these structures stand in the middle of the taiga, which supplies lumber for construction throughout the nation. It seemed the people here were lazy, or they thought of themselves as temporary inhabitants.

It was late May, and the mud in the zone was so deep that trucks and even tractors couldn't enter. The garbage and the crappers had thawed out, too, inundating the zone with an unspeakable stench. Firewood for the bath and the mess hall was piled up outside the checkpoint, and every zek returning from work had to pick up a log. Zeki moved between barracks on wooden walkways, and they didn't always succeed in walking that distance without losses. There were times when boots got stuck in the mud; they had to be pulled out by hand.

It was there that I saw a clever device for chopping

wood. I remember in Mordovia, when I had to feed the stove in the hospital zone, I had a hell of a time chopping wood. Axes in the zone were forbidden, so what was I to do? Gnaw on it? That was not a problem in Valay; there was an ax, albeit without a handle. It was welded to a large metal plate, so you'd take a log and whack it against the ax. You could just about apply for a patent.

The first time we, the new guys, showed up at the mess, all the tables were occupied. We had no place to set down our bowls. We looked at one table, which seemed almost empty, just three or four people. We sat down at that table and started eating. Other zeki, old-timers, looked at us, smirking. At last one of them came up and told us: "You boys shouldn't sit at this table. It's for the fags."

So that was how it was. This disenfranchised social mass, too, has its lowest of the low, its own "untouch-ables." The homosexuals (not all of them, just the passive; the active are treated as heroes) are the most downtrodden, the most disenfranchised part of the camp population. Any zek can treat them as he pleases. They can be thrown out of the mess hall, pushed off the bunks, forced to work for the brigade at no pay. Most of these hapless souls are young; some have become homosexuals in camps for juveniles. They view humiliation as their due; they have no one to complain to.

I didn't get a chance to observe camp life in a new place. A week after my arrival, I was called into the main office and a man who identified himself as Prosecutor Kamayev from Perm handed me two official documents: one stated that upon petition from Antonov, the Nyrob KGB officer, I was being charged under Article 190-1. The other was a warrant for my arrest and placement under guard. As if I was not under guard already. Now I would be held in a cell in the inner-camp prison.

So it turned out Antonov's threats were not idle.

First I stated orally and in writing that Antonov had maliciously fabricated the case, which was something he'd threatened me with on my first day in Nyrob.

"Marchenko, just think what you are saying!" said Kamayev, doing his best to act refined, to prove me wrong without raising his voice. He is a prosecutor. He is objective. He is from the outside. He is about thirty or thirty-five, he is tidy, his teeth are white, he is outgoing. My hostility shocks him.

"Why would Antonov or I want to fabricate a case against you? We obey the law. We always go by the law."

"Yes, certainly. And thirty years ago, millions of our countrymen were all spies and saboteurs. Yes, that was the law, I know."

"What do you know? In the Soviet state nobody was ever imprisoned or executed 'for nothing.' Khrushchev began that mess with rehabilitation, and now it's up to us to clean it up."

"What a statement to hear from a prosecutor!"

"Now, I take it you will tell me you are here for no reason at all. You wouldn't have been here if not for your pen pushing."

"Pardon me, but I am here for violation of passport regulations, not for pen pushing."

"Who cares what the charges say? It takes brains to write books, too. Some writer! Eight years' education."

"As I recall, the founder of your Socialist Realism didn't have even that."

"What gives you the right to compare yourself with

Maxim Gorky! He'd gone through a school of life! A real university."

"I believe your criminal code now defines those universities as 'vagrancy.' "

"Marchenko, Marchenko, you are giving yourself away. Talking about 'your Gorky,' 'your criminal code.' So, I take it, you aren't 'ours.' "

"Could that be my crime? That I am not 'yours'? Which article would that be?"

"You know the law, I can tell right away." Kamayev changes to a purely official tone of voice. "[KGB] Operations Officer Antonov received signals that you have systematically distributed slander and lies about our system. You may familiarize yourself with these." He pulls a few papers out of a file and hands them to me.

They were "reports" from prisoners in Nyrob. Each one of them said that in the residential zone and at the construction site Marchenko was spreading slander about "our" Soviet way of life and "our" party. Evidence of such quality was readily available. There was all you could want.

Senseless banter never stops in camps for common criminals. Zeki argue about everything, politics included. You can hear all sorts of things here, from information that can be classified as state secrets to lively vignettes about intimate relations involving members of the government and the Politburo. Naturally, everyone has "the most reliable information." Just try to express doubt! Camp polemics know no limitation and, in the heat of things, arguments have been known to turn into fist-fights. It is best to steer away from such disputes. Even when the debaters turn to you as an arbiter, beware! You know that they are talking nonsense, but if you try to tell

them so, if you try to prove them wrong, they will unite against you. Just moments ago they were ready to cut each other's throat. Now they will unite to cut yours.

I remembered this from the fifties. Now, in the late sixties, I was observing exactly the same thing. There were times when the debaters turned to me. Generally I brushed them off, saying that I didn't know. Invariably, that triggered the same reaction: "Cocksucker! Reads all the time and doesn't know shit!"

There I would be, in bed in the barrack, reading. In the aisle, two zeki are growing hoarse from insults and arguing. One of them shakes my bed. "Hey, deaf one, you tell us it's true that in real life Lenin was a pederast."

What do you say to that?

Often I wondered if that sort of thing was a provocation. Except that I knew the camps and their inhabitants all too well. Such banter was the norm in every prison, in every camp.

"You, DEAF ONE, you're up to your dick in books. You tell us it's true that Minister of Culture Furtseva spreads her legs for everyone in the government."

I am saved by Viktor, a zek whose bed is to my right.

"Who needs her? It's only in the newspapers that she looks so young and attractive. Brezhnev gets young girls. Komsomol members."

"Listen," I say. "Now you're saying what comes to mind from nothing to do, but when they get you, you'll blame it on everyone else, just to save your hide."

"They don't get you for blabbing unless you've been to a university. All I got is ten years' education!" That's said with complete certainty that it's the way it really is.

Should I have tried to enlighten him, to explain that

anyone could be jailed, regardless of his level of education? Should I have told him that I had done time with some guys with five or six years' education who wound up in a camp for politicals on Article 70 for telling jokes? Now that would indeed have constituted agitation, propaganda, fabrications, slander, the entire bouquet for Article 190-1, or 70.

Considering that zeki in the camp for criminals are guided by the principle "Better you die today, and I tomorrow," it doesn't take much for the KGB operative to put together a case on Article 190-1. He can always get hold of a few provocateurs who, for a parcel, a visit, or early release, would give any testimony against anyone. The most important thing is that because of senseless chatter, the KGB has just about every zek on the hook, and it all can be used in blackmail. As zeki themselves later told me, that's precisely what Antonov did when he was cooking up my case.

My spurious case, manufactured by Antonov, happened to rely on an impenetrable mass of "witness" testimony. "Marchenko stated numerous times," "always slandered," "I heard myself," and that's all the proof required. Article 190-1, which includes written as well as oral "fabrications," allows trials for words, for sounds that leave no material trace. So if two men say you're drunk, and you aren't, you still have to go sleep it off.

Of course, given the low level of legal sophistication on the part of Antonov and his witnesses ("low" may be too charitable; "zero" or "negative" is more appropriate), the case had donkey ears all over it. One would have thought Prosecutor Kamayev might have noticed them. The case didn't hold together; the depositions didn't jibe. One witness says that on such and such a date in January

167

Marchenko said this and that; another quotes me from another date. How can they remember in May what I said in January, and on what day I said it?

Most depositions were judgmental: "slandered," "fabricated," "maligned." And those that contained factual material were enough to make one laugh, albeit involuntarily. "Marchenko stated that in *Doctor Zhivago* Pasternak accurately depicted Soviet women, saying that they are bowlegged and their stockings are all twisted up." Someone's brains are all twisted up, either that guy's or Antonov's. He had dictated this, no doubt. I never discussed Pasternak or Sinyavsky with anyone in the camps, and I certainly didn't repeat the idiocy printed in the newspapers. I recalled that witness. Not too long before, frothing at the mouth, he had been shouting to his neighbor that in the United States they speak American and in England, English, and that "any fool understands this."

I pointed out the nonsensical depositions to Kamayev.

"So why is it that everyone's speaking ill of you?"

"I don't know if everyone is. It's just that Antonov included only the depositions he wanted."

"You mean to say that there were other depositions? Marchenko, all the depositions are included in the case, and all protocols are numbered. That's the law," said Kamayev with considerable self-importance.

Among other things, I explained to Kamayev that everything regarding *Doctor Zhivago* was pure nonsense. I had just read that novel, so I remembered what was in there and what wasn't. The witness, of course, hadn't read it, so he was saying God knows what, and attributing it to me.

About six weeks later, before the trial, I was allowed

to review the prosecution's case. I started looking for that deposition, but couldn't find it.

"Where could it be?" I asked Kamayev.

"In its place, of course, where else? Why do you need to see it? You seem to remember it well enough."

I leafed through the case once again, but it wasn't there. Other testimony was missing, too. It said I "praised American technology and slanderously stated that the Americans would whip our asses and be the first on the moon." When we'd first discussed it, I'd told Kamayev that even though that testimony was false, I did indeed have a high opinion of American technology and that I thought the Americans would indeed be the first on the moon. That conversation was in May or June. By July, when I was reviewing the case, American astronauts had walked on the surface of the moon. The protocol of that interrogation was now missing from my case files. Where could it have gone?

"We'll find it, we'll find it, we'll find it in no time," muttered the prosecutor, leafing through the case and casting glances at my Moscow defense attorney, Dina Isaakovna Kaminskaya. He knew that the protocol wouldn't turn up. I could see that in his face. "That means there's no such testimony, Marchenko," he said. "You must have made a mistake."

So that was it. "That's the law."

Incidentally, while I was held in the investigations cell in Valay, I had the opportunity to observe Kamayev's other side. Zeki in the inner-camp prison had learned that a prosecutor was in the camp, and started demanding that he come over and see them. They had some complaints to make. Every day I heard them scream, "Bring in that prosecutor! Get him over here!" The guards retorted with a mighty stream of expletives. Once, in the corridor, I heard the voice of the prosecutor: "Want a prosecutor? Fuck your mother to death!"

Kamayev demonstrated a cussing proficiency no less impressive than that of prisoners and guards.

AFTER TWO WEEKS in pretrial detention, they sent me back to Solikamsk.

First, they took me to Nyrob by truck, then by voronok from Nyrob to Solikamsk. The voronok was locked; the "box" into which I was stuffed was latched and locked, too. It was dark inside, not a crack of light. The voronok stopped, budged, stopped again; by that I concluded that we had driven up on a ferry. That had to be Cherdyn. Now we'd be crossing the Vishera River.

It's an unpleasant sensation, crossing a river locked up in a box inside a voronok. I've heard the Ministry of Internal Affairs has a directive that requires that at river crossings voronok doors be kept open, in case of emergency. I don't know if such a directive really exists, or if it's someone's fantasy. In either case, sitting in a tight, metal-covered box is unpleasant in the extreme. You can just picture the voronok rolling off the ferry, with you locked inside that metal box. Anyone who has ridden in our *voronki* knows all about their locks and latches. Even under normal circumstances, closing and opening them is a problem; the guard does a lot of pushing and pulling before the lock clicks. If the voronok started rolling, the guard, too, would be in danger; there isn't a chance he would bother undoing the locks.

In the camps you hear stories about voronki sinking with convicts inside; invariably, the convicts perished.

Besides the transit prison, Solikamsk, like any self-respecting city, had a regular jail. It was in a former monastery. All they did was take down the domes.

At first I was alone in a three-man cell. On my fourth or fifth day there, I got company, a young guy of about twenty-two. He walked in, looking scared, glancing at me with such fear that at first I took him for a madman. Later he told me what had really happened: the head of the regimen had told him that as punishment for a fight, he would transfer him to a cell with a zek tiger so fierce that he'd eat him alive and leave no bones.

"The shit he told me, I couldn't sleep two nights, that's how scared I was," my cell mate said, laughing. "He said you'd been in five times, all of them for the big stuff, murders and all!"

KAMAYEV DIDN'T appear too interested in discussing the case. He liked to talk "without inclusion into the protocol," just chat. The subject discussed was always the same: Why did you write all that? Who asked you to stick your nose into it? His conclusion was always the same, too: that I won't see the outside.

One day I got taken out of a cell, pushed into a voronok, and taken someplace. The drive wasn't long. We pulled into the railroad station, straight up to a prison train. As always, all the cells were filled, but I was treated like royalty. They put me in a three-man cell all by myself. Those three-man cells—with steel doors outside the bars—were used for the unruly passengers. But I was alone, and that counted for something! Actually, at first there were four of us, three guards and I. They ordered me to undress; then they conducted a search, all by the book. "Kneel down! Spread the buttocks! Lift up the balls!" They felt me out; then, before returning my clothes, they broke up my piece of bread.

Why all the honors? Where were they taking me? Not

out of the country? Making sure I didn't smuggle out a bottle of Stolichnaya for the capitalists?

No, they took me to Perm, that was all. But they remained vigilant. On arrival, all the passengers were lined up in a column next to the railroad car, the short-termers in front, the especially dangerous recidivists behind, next to the guards and the German shepherds. To the surprise of everyone in the column, I got put in the back, behind the striped ones. A guard fastened me to himself with handcuffs.

It seemed they were either scared of me (as of a death-row convict with nothing to lose) or trying to protect me. What were they up to?

At the Perm prison they once again loaded me into a truck, which took me to yet another destination. I looked around. Some people were wearing white coats, others, pajamas. Sure thing, it was a psychiatric hospital. They took me without my belongings; that meant it was an evaluation, at least for now. What a procedure! It was my fourth trial, but the evaluation was my first.

In a big room I am invited to sit at a table, facing five or six doctors, men and women. Two men, one prison officer and one in plain clothes, are shifting around behind my back.

The conversation is conducted by a middle-aged woman. "Do you know where you are?" she asks. "Why are you here? Do you consider yourself sick or normal?"

My answers are curt. I am aggravated by her tone of voice, the shifting of the men behind me, the game of medical objectivity they are trying to draw me into. I am certain that if they have decided to put me in a mental institution, they will get the doctors' blessings to do it, and if they have decided to put me in a camp, they'll put me in the camp, even if I am a hundred percent nuts. So why take part in their game?

"I refuse to talk to you because you will write any evaluation demanded of you," I say, playing a game of my own.

"If you do not respond to our questions, it will mean that you are ill, that you are mentally ill."

"With an appropriate directive from above, you'll find me mentally ill even if I respond."

"Do you consider yourself so important and outstanding that your fate is determined 'above'?"

"That's it. So you are welcome to diagnose two manias, of grandeur and of persecution."

"I am not an investigator, I'm a doctor. You don't have to talk to investigators, if that's what you wish. But we, the doctors, have nothing to do with your case!"

"So what's the 'case' that you have in your hands?" I point at a thick file in front of her. "And why are these people here?" I nod at the officer and the plainclothesman behind me.

The woman continues to ask questions, looking into the file. "What do you think of the events in Czechoslovakia?" "What is your opinion of the living standard in the West?" "Do you believe there is freedom of the press in the USSR?"

"Pardon me, do you always ask such questions? And how do the answers influence your conclusions? Let us suppose, for instance, that I told you that there is freedom of the press in the USSR. You'd conclude I'm nuts, and I wouldn't argue."

The expert changes the subject. "Do you read newspapers? And what about books? Which writers do you like?"

"Herzen, Shchedrin, Uspensky, Gogol, Dostoyevsky ..."

"Why is it that you like only last-century writers?"

"No, I like modern ones, too."

"Whom?" She perks up.

"I will not answer this question. It is part of the case against me." (Actually, witnesses said that besides my "praises" for Pasternak, I had propagandized for Solzhenitsyn and, believe it or not, Aksyonov. I confess, I hadn't read Vasily Aksyonov then. I had no idea who that criminal writer might be. But, thanks to the KGB officer Antonov, I read him after the camps. He is a good writer, but what was it that Antonov didn't like about him? Or was he already on the KGB list?)

Looking through the case in July, I saw the report of the psychiatric evaluation: "Psychopathic personality. Sane." So my little experiment had supported my hypothesis, that no matter what I did at the evaluation, the decision had been made in advance. As much as I acted like a nut and a schizo, the evaluation said, "Sane. Welcome to the camps."

AFTER THE evaluation, I was locked up for two weeks in Perm. There, my cell mate told me an amusing story about himself.

He, too, had been in a few times. Now he was accused of diverting state-owned materials, a substantial amount of them, to the black market. He worked as an artist and decorator at a club. He had previous convictions and was facing another term; meanwhile, his investigator was working on another case, which he couldn't crack. It was a store robbery. So the investigator decided to offer my cell mate a deal: he would take responsibility for the robbery, and the investigator would use his connections in court to assure him a minimum punishment.

"First I told him to shove it," my cell mate said. "But then it occurred to me that the investigator could get himself fucked on that deal. When the store got broken into, I was out of town on business, and I had papers to prove it. The investigator didn't know it."

At the next interrogation the investigator once again offered the deal. The guy wavered a bit, just for show, then added a few conditions: bring me half a liter of vodka and food to chase it with, and I take the rap for the store; one case more, one case fewer, what's the difference when it's the camps all the same?

Later that day, the investigator called him. As soon as the guard left, he opened his briefcase and pulled out a bottle of vodka, sausage, cheese, candy, cigarettes, and a prepared confession. The zek drank the vodka, then signed the confession, not even reading it. On the way back to the cell he made it look like he was drunker than he really was. He was thrown in a punishment cell, a doctor was called in, and he documented the state of intoxication. The KGB officer and the disciplinary officer ran in. "Where did you get the vodka?" So he told the whole story. In the morning he was transferred from the punishment cell to mine. He hadn't seen his old investigator since; they gave him a new one.

I recalled a similar story. A massive campaign had been under way to get prisoners to confess voluntarily to unsolved crimes. Every camp had a poster: "A CONFESSION LEADS TO A LENIENT PUNISHMENT." Zeki were repeatedly told about cases in which someone had served a term, then, just before release, been rearrested for another crime and gotten another sentence. The moral of the story: had he confessed, he would have served it all at once. That propaganda isn't too effective. Most criminals are prone to trust their luck. But in Nyrob, one of our convicts decided to "confess." He had heard that one of his neighbors in the barrack took the rap for a crime he didn't commit, also a robbery of a store. Actually that robbery had been committed by the first convict, but his guilt was never uncovered.

So he went to Antonov, "confessed," wrote whatever he was told to write, and got the standard camp remuneration, an extra parcel, or a couple extra rubles to spend at the prison store. But the case was never reopened; after all, someone had already taken the rap. So for our zek, "taking the road to rehabilitation" and "clearing his conscience" was a risk-free undertaking.

By THE END of the investigation I was sent from the Perm Prison back to Nyrob for face-to-face interrogations. Naturally, I learned where we arrived and why only after we got there: an inmate is moved around like an object, without being informed of the destination. Once again, I was transported "with honors," by plane from Solikamsk to Nyrob. The plane was small, a three-seater, so besides the pilot and me there was room for only one guard. He was an officer, no less. Before takeoff I was handcuffed, then the cuffs were tied to the seat with my own belt.

"I am not planning to jump without a parachute," I said.

"That's all right. Let's play it safe."

Nobody bothered me as I looked at the taiga under the plane's wing. The wing was near and I could watch it vibrate from the rumbling of the engine and the on-coming airstream.

We flew low. A river was darting and turning under us. In places it reflected light, like a mirror; in places it was a dark line on the background of green. Its shores were lined with felled trees prepared to be sent down-stream, but for some reason abandoned and rotting for years. That was a regular sight at all taiga rivers. Except the view from a plane was wider, so the impression was more grim.

THE SPECTACLE of face-to-face interrogations began.

It was a sad sight, and I felt pity for some of the "wit-nesses." Others were inept to the point of being amus-ing. By their behavior, I could easily tell provocateurs from those who had gotten tangled up in Antonov's nets.

Andreyev, Sapozhnikov, and Nikolayev had sold themselves to Antonov. They were nonchalant. They didn't remember their own "testimony" given in the in-terrogation, and that didn't bother them in the least.

Kamayev reads the interrogation protocols:

"Witness, is this what you testified at an interroga-tion?"

"That's it, that's it. That's what I said."

Sapozhnikov is their trump card: he has ten years' education. A witness like that looks more reliable. He is straining, puffing, trying to pull something out of his skull, but nothing comes out. Helplessly, he looks at Kamayev and Antonov, waiting for cues.

"Well"—Antonov cannot bear the wait—"didn't Mar-chenko say at work and in the barracks that the living standard abroad is higher than in the Soviet Union?"

"Yes, yes." Sapozhnikov picks up eagerly. "Now I recall. He said many times that they live better than us. I kept trying to tell him, to prove him wrong, but he just went on slandering."

"Where did I say they live better? In which country? In Ethiopia?" I ask.

"What's the difference?" answers Sapozhnikov, his eyes on Antonov.

"Marchenko, you behave incorrectly!" warns Kamayev, turning to me. "You must be facing me at all times. Do not look at the witness. Questions must be asked only through me. Sapozhnikov, continue!"

Sapozhnikov is unable to recall anything. "Why don't you write down what you need, and I'll sign it," he offers.

At times Kamayev and Antonov, taking advantage of my poor hearing, were coaching witnesses. I could not hear them, but could read their lips. More often than not they read interrogation protocols, and witnesses nodded in agreement.

In one such instance, I get up from the chair, excuse myself, and walk out to the corridor, saying to Kamayev that I will not take part in such face-to-face interrogations.

Antonov lunges after me. He grabs me by the collar, twisting it with one hand, and pounds me under the ribs with the other. I am starting to choke; the collar has stiffened around my neck. I get a powerful urge to poke my finger in Antonov's eye, to kick him, to fight him off rather than passively endure this humiliation. Thank God I don't get a chance. Kamayev walks up to us in the corridor.

"It's enough. He's had enough. Leave him." ·

Antonov lets me go, and pushes me into the room, hissing in my ear, "You just try to blow the whistle. Just try it." He calls in two guards, who now stand in the doorway at the ready.

"Now we'll put a straitjacket on you, and you'll shit and piss," he screams, wiping sweat off his brow. "You won't just sit there like a little darling, you'll sign everything all by yourself!"

Even today I cannot recall this calmly.

Kamayev sits there smiling. "Marchenko, remember, nobody was choking you. Nobody was beating you."

The face-to-face interrogations continued. Now I wasn't taking any part in them; I even tried not to listen. It would be easier that way. Seeing my complete indifference, Kamayev and Antonov were trying to egg me on, talking about extraneous subjects.

"No, Marchenko, you should have been smarter. You write a book, and what's it done for you? Your fame's out there someplace, but you're right here, in the camps, and here you'll stay. Till you rot. So you've named some names. Who's afraid of that? Go ahead. So what if the BBC talks about us, or even Radio Liberty. You know our names. We aren't hiding them."

That subject kept cropping up.

"Go ahead, tell the United Nations about us. We aren't scared."

I can just picture those faithful sons of the Fatherland, their ears up against the shortwave radios, hoping that the "hostile voices" would not forget their names.

This peculiar vanity is typical among lower-level officials. Larisa tells me she, too, encountered a fame seeker. He was head of the Chuna militia.

"You think I am afraid of the Voice of America broadcasting about me?" he said to her once. "I am not afraid. My name is Vladimirov."

"Whom do you dislike more, the militia or the KGB?" he asked Larisa at the same meeting.

He was visibly pleased to hear that Larisa views the militia with loyalty and that she respects its function in society. It seemed the opinion of a political exile was something he needed for his self-respect.

18

AFTER A PROCESSION of zeki, the prosecutor pulled out his trump card, and an ace at that: the testimony of a civilian employee named Rybalko. He would pick me out of a lineup.

"Here you have it, a free man, in no way dependent on Antonov. And he, too, is ready to testify against you," Antonov says with obvious self-importance.

"I don't know any Rybalko."

"But he knows you very well indeed. You will have a chance to see that."

The lineup was strictly by the book: there were three witnesses, all of them zeki. Kamayev, as a prosecutor, presided over the procedure. I didn't quite understand Antonov's role, but I could see him making the preparations, going through logistics, organizing. There were three chairs by the opposite wall; two were already occupied by zeki. Antonov told me to sit in the third. Rybalko's function was to point out Marchenko and tell all he knew about that sinister character.

Antonov walks out to bring in Rybalko.

I walk up and say, "I request a delay in bringing in the witness."

"What's the problem?" asks the surprised Kamayev.

"I would like to sit in another chair."

"Go right ahead," says Kamayev, feigning impartiality.

I change places with one of the zeki, then ask him, "Why don't we exchange shoes till the game's over?"

The zek readily agrees, and we swap shoes. I get his summer shoes; he gets my boots. "Would you hold my hat?" I ask the other zek, the one on the right.

That done, I turn to Kamayev. "I am ready."

Kamayev nods to the guard to open the door. A darkish man of medium height, wearing civilian clothes, walks in first. I cannot recognize him. I could swear I haven't seen him before. Antonov comes in after him. He doesn't look in my direction, and deliberately turns his back to the three of us, facing Kamayev. There's a cigarette in his mouth.

Kamayev instructs Rybalko.

"Do you understand everything, Witness Rybalko?"

"Yes, everything."

"Now face the three inmates and point out the one who was slandering the party and the government. Point out which of these three is Marchenko."

Rybalko turns to us and, without hesitation, points to the zek with whom I have just swapped shoes.

"Here he is. Here's Marchenko. I recognize him. He was the one who said that . . ."

And he goes on, repeating what was in the protocols of his interrogation: when he, a master, came to the construction site, he heard the inmates engage in political disputes. One of the inmates, that one, Marchenko (he once again points at the man next to me), always slandered the Soviet power, praised the foreign way of life, and stated that there is no freedom of speech, freedom of the press, or freedom of assembly. On one occasion Marchenko referred to our assistance to the Czechoslovak people as "occupation." That was the time that he and I went at each other so bad that we were barely pulled apart by other zeki. He also stated that it was the Soviet government that was to blame for the armed conflict with China over Damansky Island.

"Rybalko, would you please look again?" Kamayev tries to get his attention. "Could you be mistaken? Is this really Marchenko, or is it another one? Which one is he?"

Rybalko takes this warning as a hint that he needs to reaffirm his identification more emphatically.

"Yes, yes, that's him. Marchenko. I remember him clearly."

"Could you be mistaken, Rybalko? Look carefully! Do you really recognize Marchenko?"

Rybalko is working in earnest.

"How can I be mistaken? I almost slugged him across the mouth, back when he was slandering. I'll remember him all my life and never forget him!"

"Now, how will I prove that I am not a camel?" half-whispers the zek who has been so clearly identified by Rybalko.*

Now Antonov turns around to look at us. Seeing that I am sitting in the middle, not where he left me, and that Rybalko is pointing his finger at someone other than me, he turns deep red, temporarily losing the gift of speech. The cigarette trembles on his lip.

"I am not Marchenko," says the zek, putting an end to the charade. "That one's Marchenko."

---

*A reference to a joke: In 1937, during Stalin's purges, a hare is running down the street screaming, "The camels are being castrated! The camels are being castrated!"
"So why are you running? You are a hare."
"Yes, sure, they catch you, castrate you, then go ahead and prove to them you are not a camel." (Trans.)

Puzzled, Rybalko looks at Antonov.

"That's how you get a term," says the zek to my right. "And you won't know what for."

"Yes," says Kamayev. "You were mistaken, Rybalko. You were pointing at the wrong man. And didn't recognize Marchenko."

Finally, Rybalko understands his error. Breaking through the laughter of the witnesses and the men in the lineup, he can do little more than repeat, "Yes! Yes! Now I recognize his voice! That's him!"

"How did you recognize my voice? I've been silent all through this."

"I recognize him. I do!"

Kamayev shouts at everyone to cut out the laughter. I demand that he draft a protocol of identification, making the following notation: "Rybalko failed to recognize Marchenko and pointed at the wrong man."

It was the only document I signed.

Finally, the zek to my right adds another detail. He'd been trying to say something since they first led Rybalko into the room, but Kamayev had ordered him to shut up. Now he made his statement: "What kind of a lineup is it if I am well acquainted with Rybalko, and he knows me by name and appearance? He was head of our guard unit; he was the one who took us to work every day."

"So is Antonov fabricating the case or isn't he?" I ask Kamayev.

"It was Rybalko who failed to recognize you. What does Antonov have to do with it?" replies the prosecutor.

On the way to the cell, I am congratulated by the guard: "Now you're off the hook. Antonov didn't get a fucking thing."

Later, in the corridor to the inner-camp prison, he

joyfully informs the duty officer and another guard: "This one fucked them over real good. Like in the movies."

NOT EVERYONE at the face-to-face interrogations behaved as impudently as Rybalko and Sapozhnikov. Some acted ensnared, not looking at me or Antonov or Kamayev; others answered questions unwillingly, forcing themselves, angrily barking out, "So, he said it!" "I don't remember. Could be." It was clear that Antonov had those men on the hook, because of their blabbering, or for some other infraction. Provocateurs like Andreyev and Sapozhnikov helped them become false witnesses, and though they surrendered, it was obvious they weren't getting any pleasure from lying to my face. I almost have to feel sorry for them.

Every one of them was lying. I don't know if it's even possible to believe it: there wasn't one word of truth in their testimony. Not one.

Of course, I wouldn't be able to demonstrate this to the court. I didn't even hope to. But, what was worse, my friends would probably think that I'd acted carelessly and imprudently in the camps; I doubted they would understand that the whole case, from first word to last, was a shameless lie. After all, the accusation was based on what I really think, on the opinions and views that I indeed hold. Yes, I knew that in the United States the living standard was higher than in the USSR. Yes, I thought we were far behind in technological innovations. Yes, I saw that we had no freedom of speech, no freedom of the press, and certainly, no freedom of assembly. And, yes, I regarded the "fraternal help" to Czechoslovakia in 1968 as occupation and aggression, as defined by international law.

It's all true. It's just that I never said anything of the sort to anyone in the camps.

So at one interrogation I faced my old bunk mate. He was from Moscow, formerly a taxi driver, now a classic criminal: a drunk and a drug addict ready to steal a friend's last ruble in a card game, a known stoolie, and a frequent visitor in Antonov's office. I recall him screaming in the barracks about the Czechs and the Slovaks: "Those whores, strangle them all, one by one! We liberate them and they turn on us! What the fuck do we waste our time with them for? Get a thousand bulldozers and level it all. Down to the roots!"

Such calls for bloodshed wouldn't be regarded as grounds for prosecution. It is precisely such patriot-criminals who make up the foundation of our ideological unity.

To be honest, most men in the barracks agreed with his "criticism from the right," while the rest simply showed no interest in any events removed more than 200 meters from their asses.

In the winter and spring of 1969, dispatches from Czechoslovakia were the first thing I turned to when I opened up the newspapers. The fate of that country became as important to me as the fate of my own people. But there was no one in the camps I could share my concerns with. After reading my newspapers, I usually left the barrack and walked up and down the path I had made for myself. I never shared my despair with anyone. I returned to the barrack after taps, so I could lie down and fall asleep without seeing or hearing all that was repulsive around me.

So the drug addict testified: "Marchenko called the deployment of Soviet troops an 'occupation.' I tried to set him straight, but he kept on slandering." And how much that looks like the truth! Except why would I tell that lowlife what I thought of the policies of the Communist Party of the Soviet Union when I wouldn't tell him what I thought of yesterday's dinner in the camp's mess hall?

Still, how could I discredit such testimony? How could I say, no, I am not like that, I am not opposed to policies of the party, my thinking's correct, as any Soviet person's thinking should be? I couldn't do that.

So there I was, at Kamayev's interrogation, disputing testimony.

"Now, Marchenko, you've written that yourself in your letter about Czechoslovakia," Kamayev jeers.

READING the taxi driver's testimony with me, my attorney glances at me, feeling out my reaction.

"Dina Isaakovna, it's all lies, like everything else."

Cautiously, she hints, "Anatoly, could it possibly be that you have said something like it? Maybe not exactly those words, but in essence . . ."

It's hard to believe that it's all lies, especially considering that Dina Isaakovna, too, probably knows about my open letter to *Rude Pravo* and other newspapers.

If your views diverge from the current demands of the "CPSU line," you find yourself in a no-win situation. Soviet leaders tell the world incessantly, "In the USSR no one is persecuted for his views." Soviet law, they claim, guarantees a citizen's right to hold any views. That's true, as long as no one knows about those views. Potentially, any two interlocutors are two witnesses who would confirm that you conducted agitation and propaganda, spread slander, and committed other "unlawful acts."

Let's suppose I accepted the rules of the game and

agreed to keep my thoughts to myself. That would make me not just an ordinary enemy, but a deceitful, cowardly enemy. "He votes aye, but thinks nay," as the late Iosiv Vissarionovich used to say. How do you find such a deceitful enemy and render him harmless? Actually, any method will do, and during the history of the USSR some methods have been preferred over others. Lenin and Dzerzhinski favored provocation: everyone knows that former officers, the clergy, and the liberal intelligentsia are all outsiders, and thus potential enemies. So they should be called in and forced into actions and statements for which they could justifiably be shot or sent to Solovki. The Stalin clique, by contrast, didn't concern itself with finding or fabricating justifications: they killed any offending thought in embryo (or even earlier), together with its potential carrier.

Today we have returned to "Leninist justice," yet we have taken some lessons from the later epoch of creative Marxism.

ON THE OUTSIDE, in 1968, for one reason or another they found it uncomfortable to try me for open expression of my views. Then the bosses at Nyrob learned about those views through some extraneous means—with the help of telepathy, the KGB information service—an inner voice told them; that same inner voice told them what was on my mind. So the provocations and the fabricated case would work! After all, I wouldn't renounce my views. In this country all crime is punished, one way or another.

So freedom of expression is most precisely described by a new joke:

"Comrade jurist, tell me, do I have a right to ..."

"Yes, comrade, you do."

"Excuse me, you didn't let me finish, do I have a right to . . ."

"Yes, you have that right. . . ."

"Please, let me finish. *Can I* . . ."

"No, comrade, you *cannot*."

That's how it works: you have your rights, but you cannot.

My case had one amusing characteristic: no one accused me of talking about camps and prisons. It seems that I was burning their ears with banter about some faraway Czechoslovakia with its "Czechoslovakian" language, about freedom of expression (and not even unprintable expression at that), about some mysterious Pasternak-Aksyonov, without ever uttering a word about what was so near to them: reduced rations, escapes, suicides. That would have made effective grounds for propaganda. Nonetheless, Antonov and Kamayev could not trust even their most faithful stoolies and provocateurs with information about my alleged statements on that subject.

Also, consider the intellectual level and the form of the "falsities" attributed to me: "Communists have sucked out all my blood!" I am alleged to have shouted in a punishment cell. "I won't work for the Communists!" Both statements are classified as "slanderous slogans." I must say that both these slogans are often shouted in the camps, prisons, and punishment cells. It's an accepted way of expressing displeasure, a reaction to virtually anything: say, you didn't get your smokes (or had them taken away), you've been transferred to another brigade, your warm socks have been confiscated in a search, you weren't able to get morphine. Naturally, nobody pays any attention to such screams. But when the time came to start my case, Antonov got the only

189

"slogan" he knew: "Communists have sucked out all my blood!" It's humiliating to try proving that I never said anything of the sort.

What sort of a position could my defense attorney take at the trial? I would keep repeating, "That's a lie. And that's a lie. Nothing of the sort ever happened." I knew the case was fabricated. The witnesses knew it, the prosecutor knew it. But the defense attorney has to rely on the facts, which in this case did not—and could not—exist on either side. It was all their word against mine. What would my attorney be able to do in the face of that gang? So I decided to waive representation rather than put Dina Isaakovna in an idiotic situation. I would defend myself. The outcome was predetermined anyway.

19

THE PROCEEDINGS were open; it was a show trial, just about. On a weekday, the library where it was being held was filled with zeki, with guards and officers mixed in.

I didn't expect anything new at the trial and prepared myself to hear what I had read in the protocols and heard at the face-to-face interrogations. Yet it seems I had overestimated the degree to which the spectacle had been rehearsed and the diligence of its producer. The proceedings held several pleasant surprises.

For one thing, the "slanderous slogans" testimony fell apart. When I had read it in the prosecution's folder, the accusation was based on depositions of four witnesses, including Sedov, a zek trusty at the inner-camp prison; two guards; and zek Dmitryenko, who was repairing the stove in the corridor. They said that on such and such a date, every time the feed hole in his door was opened, Marchenko shouted out those "slogans."

I hadn't seen any of them at face-to-face interrogations. Now, at the trial, they called Dmitryenko.

"Witness Dmitryenko, do you know the accused?"

"No, this is the first time I have seen him."

"What? And your deposition?"

"Yes, I wrote one under Antonov's orders. I heard those shouts, but didn't know who was shouting. Antonov told me, 'It was Marchenko shouting. Write it that way.' Now I know that it was not Marchenko, but another inmate, from another cell. If it pleases the court, I will name that man. He is present at these proceedings."

No, the prosecutor wasn't interested in the name of the real "guilty party." The court did not choose to pursue that subject. I could have asked, but why would I want to bring troubles onto a zek I didn't know? I wouldn't have done so even if he had shouted that it was I, not the Communists, who had sucked his blood out.

"Witness Dmitryenko, besides you, who heard those slogans?" the judge asked.

"It was Operations Officer Antonov, together with Inmate Sedov, who were convincing me to write that deposition. Sedov also wrote such a deposition. Recently the camp administration petitioned for his pardon, and he has been released from the camp."

Sedov had been pardoned! He was thrown into inner-camp prison (where he also worked) for systematic and malicious violations of the regime, and his six-month term in inner-camp prison wasn't up yet. Now he was not just out of his cell, he was out of the camps. He'd earned it! I wonder what Antonov said in his petition for Sedov's pardon.

I asked the court to enter Dmitryenko's exact testimony in the record. I also asked to call the inmates who had been held in the inner-camp prison with me. Their depositions were not in the case. That meant Antonov either got lazy or hadn't managed to work them over.

"Whom precisely would you want to call?" asked Judge Khrenovsky. "What are their names?"

"I don't know their names."

"So how do you suggest we find your witnesses?"

"They are easy to find. There's a registry for punishment cells and the inner-camp prison. It has their names, dates, the hours and minutes they were there."

The court decided to satisfy my request, then adjourned till the next day. I was led away to the cell. Here, in the evening, I once again saw Dmitryenko. He was the one who brought in the food. Until then I hadn't seen the face of the man who brought the food around. He'd shove a bowl into my hands through the hole in the door; I saw only his hand, which he would promptly pull away. Now I realized that Dmitryenko knew that it was Marchenko in the cell, the very Marchenko he had informed on, falsely at that. That Marchenko, God forbid, might poke his eyes out or throw hot grub in his face. In the camps that's a time-honored form of revenge. Now Dmitryenko saw that "that very Marchenko" wasn't as he'd imagined, which meant we weren't enemies anymore. He stood by the feeder, smiling.

"Forgive me, friend, I really didn't know. Sedov, that lowlife, and the KGB officer got me into it. 'Marchenko,' they said. 'Marchenko, write that it was Marchenko.' "

The guard rushed him off and shut the feed hole in the door, but I could still hear Dmitryenko: "Sedov knew what he was doing. He sold himself to the KGB officer for a pardon!"

I was in a fine mood that evening. Dmitryenko had spoiled their show. Besides, I got an extraordinary food parcel with fried chicken, grapes, cakes, and an enormous, juicy pear. All of it was brought to me from Moscow by a young defense attorney who came to represent me in place of Dina Isaakovna.* I rejected her help and did my best to make her understand my reasons. I felt

---

*Marchenko's Moscow friends hired the attorney to observe the trial and inform them about it. (Trans.)

awkward; she had come this far only to hand me a chicken and a pear. But the awkwardness did not ruin my appetite.

She gave me the parcel right in the courtroom, and, returning to the cell under guard, I carried a mesh bag with chicken legs sticking out of it; I put the grapes and the pear on top, so I wouldn't smash them. As I was being led to the cell, a sergeant happened by, the same one who had delivered me to Nyrob from Solikamsk, abusing me all the way. He hadn't fed me, and when I had to urinate, he'd stopped at a place with people around; he was fat and had a foul mouth. The sergeant immediately spotted objects unusual for these parts: the chicken, a pear, and grapes. His eyes popped out.

"What the fuck! Where's this from?"

"Presented to me by the court."

"On what right! Not allowed!"

"You drove me here without dinner; did you ask me about rights? Now you see a zek has a chicken and you remember rights!"

"Don't let him take it into his cell," the sergeant said to the guard. "I'll go make sure they take it from him. Hold him up while I'm gone."

"Get out of here," blurted the guard. "Go back to Solikamsk and give your orders."

And the guard escorted me to the cell.

Just to be sure, I ate all I could before they took it away. It's a zek rule: grab whatever falls in your hands, don't let it drop. Camp rules and habits seep into one's nature; you aren't rid of them even on the outside. I remember when Leonid Rendel got out after doing nine years, back in 1967. Moscow friends gave him a party, a dinner with various delicacies. Someone asked him,

"Lyonya, what do you think about ——?" I can't recall what it was.

Preparing to give a serious, exhaustive answer, Rendel thoroughly licked his spoon on both sides (they call it "burnishing" in the camps) and put it in the breast pocket of his new suit. A zek always carries his spoon in the only pocket of his prison-camp vestments.

Once, at a checkout in a large self-service grocery store in Moscow, I raised my arms, opening my sides for patting down, like at a zone checkpoint. This gesture stunned everyone around me; still, I didn't immediately realize what had happened.

And in 1973, when Larisa and I registered our marriage, a comic scene took place. Our witnesses were Lyuda Alekseyeva and Kolya Williams. He had done his time under Stalin. An usher with a ribbon over her shoulder decorously invited us: "Walk forward, one after another, please."

So the procession was led by the groom, that was me, with Dr. Williams, a mathematician, drifting behind, in single file. Both of us had our hands behind us. It looked like a painting, *A Walk in a Prison Yard*.

THE NEXT DAY "my" witnesses were called, the ones who'd been in a punishment cell with me. There were about twenty of them. The turnover out there is almost complete, every day. None of them confirmed that I shouted anything.

"Him? The deaf one? He never even came near the feeder hole in the door when I was there."

Twenty people in the same cell with me never heard me shout anything.

After hearing Dmitryenko and those witnesses, the

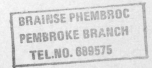

court should have expressed doubts about the rest of the case—after all, Dmitryenko had said that Antonov ordered him to write about Marchenko. That would not happen, though, of course. The trial would go on, but at least the idiotic story about the "slogans" fell through.

Suddenly, among my witnesses, my former cell mates, I saw a man I had never laid eyes on before; I swear. He was emaciated, and had a typically eastern face, an Uzbek, I guess. I would have remembered him if I had seen him. I couldn't make out his name. The unexpected always provokes suspicion; Antonov may have snuck in his own man. So I rushed in with a statement: "I have never been in the same cell with this man, and have never seen him in my life."

"I will speak for myself. Don't do it for me," the witness shot back.

For a minute or so we got into a senseless altercation: I kept repeating, "Never seen him before," and he retorted, "I will speak for myself," with his slight eastern accent.

Finally the judge cut us off and started examining the witness. What I heard next was even more alarming: he had a technician's degree and a degree from an evening institute of Marxism-Leninism. "That one will really say what they want," I said to myself.

"Which article have you been convicted under?" the judge asked.

"One ninety, section one; the term's three years."

"What?" I barely managed to scream out. "One ninety! Here! A colleague, where are you from, what for?"

The prosecutor livened up, too. "Your testimony will be extremely valuable to the court," he said, addressing the new witness.

"I understand. I will do my best," the witness agreed.

"I am always in the punishment cell since I refuse to come out and work. And I refuse to work because I am physically unable to fill work quotas. So I decided that it's better to stay hungry in a punishment cell than to be half hungry while breaking my back at work. So I was in a punishment cell at the same time with Marchenko. His shouting is all an invention. I never heard that shouting."

"Witness, why do you call it an invention?"

"It's not just me saying it. The whole camp's saying it. The guards, too."

"The court realizes that you are unable to say anything relevant to the case."

"I am able. What I say is relevant; you are saying the shouts weren't relevant, right? You know the shouts I've heard in the camp; I'm afraid to repeat them. But I never heard them from Marchenko, I've never even seen him. But I've heard them from everyone else. First I tried to stop them, but they insulted me, called me a 'Communist' or a 'Komsomolets,' as an insult. I got beat up, too."

I didn't get everything that guy said. He spoke fast, to get in as much as he could before they cut him off. I never did learn his name.

So, friend, where are you now? Did you serve out your term in a punishment cell? Did your Marxist education serve you well?

I COULDN'T hear many other witnesses, either. I couldn't make out a word from the testimony of a young soldier, a draftee sent to guard the camps. He stood close to me, and I could see he barely moved his lips. He answered with his head down, looking at his feet. Poor guy!

Many witnesses slumped into that posture, but there were also those who delivered their oratory with pleasure, though with little finesse.

"Yes, he slandered. Can't remember what he said, but it was slander, that's for certain."

"He falsely stated that in the Czechoslovak Socialist Republic, the tanks trampled freedom, but didn't say what freedom."

"I tried to convince Marchenko, but he didn't agree." That phrase, verbatim, appears in all the testimony of all the "programmed" witnesses. And they kept repeating, "He slandered, but never forced his views on others." That's a strange statement whose meaning, no doubt, was lost on those repeating it there, but it was clear to me. It meant that the instruction was to convict me under Article 190, not anything worse. And that was something to praise the Lord for.

The witnesses were so numerous that it seemed there was enough testimony to account for every day I spent at Nyrob. On such and such a day I "slandered," on another "stated," then, on another day, I "shouted." In short, I blubbered nonstop, never giving my mouth a rest. At the same time, all the witnesses portrayed me as a loner: grim, suspicious, and silent.

That, for all practical purposes, was the end. I couldn't re-create the drumbeat of the prosecutors' closing argument, not even if I wanted to. Like the prosecution's speeches at all political trials, it was a conglomeration of senseless newspaper clichés: "Under the leadership of the Communist Party," "the building of the Communist Society," "ideological-political unity," "ideological incursion of the West," "a handful of renegades"—a lot of nonsense.

All that was notable was the remark the prosecutor tailored to the audience: "Though every one of you here is serving a just punishment, you are all Soviet people, which you have demonstrated with your attitude to Marchenko's actions. Well, as they say, there is an ugly one in every family."

There wasn't much fervor in my closing argument; it was a senseless exercise. Still, I think I covered all the points: Dmitryenko's testimony, the testimony of my cell mates, Rybalko's failure to recognize me in a lineup. I also addressed the nature of the charges, the arbitrary interpretation of "deliberately false fabrications." Judge Khrenovsky stopped me several times, but I still managed to finish, returning to my original point: "The case was fabricated by Antonov and Kamayev."

They read the sentence: two years of strict-regimen camps. More lenient than I had expected. They could have slapped me with the maximum, three years, but I got a year less; or they could have found me an especially dangerous recidivist and sent me to a special camp, to the "striped ones." What am I saying! Had they been told to, they could just as easily have slapped me with Article 70, and that's up to seven years. The bosses demonstrated lenience and humanity. Should they be thanked for it?

IF ONLY they could have done it without a trial, without this comedy in which you are given a part, into which you get drawn despite yourself. If they had just issued a decree: "You are to spend two years in the camps!" But this way you could wind up with three—or all seven. Just like that, because.

The verdict said my guilt was confirmed by witnesses, this followed by a list of witnesses, regardless of what they said, even Rybalko. His testimony also "confirms . . ." As for my cell mates, their testimony didn't "disprove the guilt," since they seemed not to have heard the "slanderous slogans" shouted by Marchenko.

199

So why did they bother with this talkathon?

God damn it, what did I need all that for?

Still, I forced them to let me see the protocol of the proceedings. The law requires that all parties, including the accused, sign the protocol of the trial. As a rule he signs it without looking, not even knowing what he signs. Later he files an appeal, claiming that the court considered something or other incorrectly, which gets a response: "The materials of the trial demonstrate no grounds for reconsideration." And the defendant had signed those materials without looking.

I had no plans to appeal, but made my demands nonetheless: "I wish to see the protocol."

"What for?" grumbled Judge Khrenovsky. "You heard everything. Or is there anything that's not clear to you?"

And the Solikamsk sergeant attacked me verbally, stopping just short of using his fists; he didn't want to spend another day or two waiting for me in this hole.

In the protocols I saw what I expected. Everything was recorded slapdash, inaccurately; everything that could have been screwed up was. That's commonplace. The girls, secretaries, don't understand what they are recording. There wasn't a trace of Dmitryenko's testimony, even his name was not mentioned. Naturally, that deliberate distortion didn't originate with the secretary.

To Khrenovsky's obvious displeasure, I amended the protocol with Dmitryenko's testimony, signed it, and asked the judge to sign it, as amended.

I don't think it's that difficult to understand the psychology of a man in my situation. But the psychology of the state in such trials has always been a mystery to me.

Consider the 1930s and 1940s, when millions were dispatched to the camps, or directly into the ground. Dispatched without getting into the particulars, with no records kept, just about. Still, a colossal army of investigators and their helpers first tried to beat one thing out of their victims: "Sign this testimony. Sign the confession. Admit that you are a spy." Why? For the show trials they needed but a few dozen; meanwhile, they were trying to beat this out of millions. Some admitted, others didn't, but in the end it was all the same—every one of them got herded off to Kolyma, Vorkuta, Norilsk, or put up against a wall. Just imagine all the paper wasted, all the investigators' man-hours, all the pay they drew over twenty years. They had to be fed well, lots of calories, so they'd have the strength to knock out the prisoners' teeth. And, for the time of investigation, the prisoners had to be fed, too; that was state food, with no returns generated. Why all that trouble? I can't understand.

Today's political trials are less costly since there are fewer of them. But it's still squandered resources: for me alone, Kamayev drew his salary for three months. And I was shifted around from Valay to Solikamsk, to Perm, back to Solikamsk, to Nyrob, back to Solikamsk, back to Nyrob, then to Solikamsk again. I traveled by train, truck, and airplane. The guards had to be paid and fed. Zeki had to be taken off their jobs and dragged to interrogations, the lineup, the trial. I'll bet quarterly quotas didn't get filled, all because of me. The cost to the camp had to be high. If they'd just sentenced me right away, without a trial, without investigation, without those holdups, they'd have put me to work, and though I'm not the best worker around, I would have at least covered the costs of my upkeep (including the guards, barbed-wire depreciation, and so on).

From day one to the end, to the sentence, all parties in the case—Antonov, the prosecutor, the judge, the witnesses, myself, and those who issued the directives—were all weaving some senseless and impractical ornament, knowing that it had nothing to do with reality. Still, everyone tried to weave his part of the ornament as thoroughly and as artfully as possible.

I wonder if all these actions, these investigations, these trials serve the same purpose as some ritual dances; it's all symbolism. The repetition of the words *slander, falsity,* and others has the same function as the magic spell "Be gone, be gone, vanish." The prosecutor is the shaman, all others are the required props. It's just that I don't know if ordinary shamans preside over human sacrifices.

In the evening, a note tightly scribbled on a notebook page and rolled into the shape of a bullet was thrown through the cell feed hole. It said that Rybalko was under investigation for theft of construction materials from the work site, and that Antonov had promised to drop the case—for a price. That price was testimony against me.

Antonov caught many other witnesses the same way: if you don't testify against Marchenko, you'll be tried yourself. I've got enough on you here. Others were told: "Marchenko confessed to everything, and you are still covering up for him; we'll prosecute you for it. Everyone in the zone knows it."

The note didn't say anything I didn't know. Still, after seeing so many a man fall to disgrace during the trial, it was pleasing to receive good tidings from someone I didn't even know.

I spent much of that evening by the window. The inner-camp prison stood on a knoll, and the window gave a view of places beyond the wooden fence topped with a barbed-wire ledge, beyond the large spirals of barbed wire, beyond wire laid out in intricate patterns, with empty cans attached to it, beyond another barbed-wire fence with guard dogs chained on the other side.

About 20 meters from the dogs stood an old, half-rotted barn; sparrows raced in circles around it. They made a chirping racket, of course, but I couldn't hear the sounds, all I could do was guess.

The jackdaws weren't racing; they were dignified and businesslike. They walked the rooftop, rhythmically turning their heads. High above the barn, a large kite leisurely circled the clear predawn sky. It was hard to make out his markings, but I could see him turning his head, spotting the prey below. At times, like a rock, he dropped to the ground, just by the barn. He didn't always make it all the way down, and more often than not he spread out his mighty wings and resumed his graceful circles. Steadily, he would regain height. And as he circled upward, I got a good look at his markings: he was dark brown, a smoky brown, and the darkness of his wings was split with a bright yellow streak.

I didn't sleep that night. God knows, the sentence wasn't too bad, just two years. That term didn't scare me in the least (or so I thought that night); after all, in 1967, I had expected something much worse. In any case, I felt that I would have preferred a conviction on Article 70 and a seven-year sentence for writing the book and the open letters, that is, a conviction for something I had really done. That would have been easier to take than a two-year sentence on a fabricated case; it would not have unleashed this sense of helplessness, this gloom. Aside from the humiliation of falsehoods that are both overt and impossible to discredit, I sensed the hopelessness of my situation, my total dependence on an unseen master. He may let me out two years from now, if he is so inclined; and if he isn't, I'll get another of their "talking articles," either 190-1 or, just as easily, 70. "He said . . . " "He insisted . . . " "He slandered . . ."

That night there were moments when I felt that my term would have no end, that they would keep playing their games, adding two years here, three there, trying to get me to renounce my views and my book. That feeling of uncertainty didn't leave me for the ensuing two years of imprisonment.

AFTERWORD
BY LARISA BOGORAZ

On December 9, 1986, just before noon, I received an urgent telegram from Chistopol: YOUR HUSBAND MARCHENKO ANATOLY TIKHONOVICH PASSED AWAY IN HOSPITAL. GIVE URGENT RESPONSE ON YOUR POSSIBLE ARRIVAL. AKHMADEYEV.

The telegram came just as I was walking out the door to send my husband a parcel. A few days earlier I'd gotten a letter from him. He was asking me to send him a package of food. That meant just one thing, that his four-month hunger strike was over. A load had fallen off my shoulders. My husband's life was now out of danger. Of late, I had been getting a feeling that he would soon be free, and I hoped that in a matter of days we would be together.

The news of Anatoly's death struck me right in the heart.

On December 9, my relatives, a few friends, Anatoly's and my thirteen-year-old son, Pavel, and I left for Chistopol. All together there were nine of us. By 4:00 P.M., December 10, we stood at the gates of Chistopol Prison. We were told that Akhmadeyev, the head of the prison, was ill, and we never succeeded in meeting with him. I was received by Churbanov, the political officer, and all our further official contacts were with him only. We saw no one else. On our last day, Churbanov walked out to us outside the prison gate and, in a harsh tone, said, "You will not be received here by anyone anymore."

On the first evening we met with Almeyev, the head of the medical ward and the only doctor in the prison. But that was our only meeting with anyone on the medical staff at the prison.

We had questions, of course, and as each day passed, we had new ones: What did Anatoly Marchenko die of? What was his condition in his last few days? Did he really end his hunger strike? When? Was he conscious as he was dying? Who was with him during the last hours of his life?

Almeyev and Churbanov began with the lies, and with the lies they ended. Most of our questions received no answers at all.

Churbanov had one obvious concern: to put Marchenko's body in the ground as promptly as possible, to hold the burial the next day, at nine in the morning. We asked him to give the body to us, so we could hold the burial in Moscow, near my parents' resting place. "Inmates who die in prison are to be buried by the administration in the presence of relatives," we were told. We said that we wanted to hold a Russian Orthodox funeral, with a church service. No, again. "You will view the body in the morgue, in a coffin, prepared for burial. At that point you will have the opportunity to say farewell."

That evening we were not allowed to see the deceased or to spend the last night by the coffin.

Later we learned that the body was not left alone: three agents of the Ministry of Internal Affairs (or was it the KGB?) held vigil in the morgue's offices from dawn December 9 until the funeral. They were guarding the deceased Marchenko!

After several nighttime telegrams and calls to Moscow

and Kazan, we were allowed to delay the burial by two hours and hold a service at Chistopol's Russian Orthodox church.

Men in plain clothes, who weren't leaving us for as much as a minute, filed into the funeral bus. The bus was followed by a Gazik with our "escort." The bus was brought right up to the morgue door, like a prison van. "Everyone is ordered to sit in place! Now we will carry in the coffin," said Churbanov. He had arrived in the Gazik. But all of us got up and said we would not allow any of them to touch the coffin. We would carry it out ourselves and we would bury it ourselves. They didn't want to let us into the morgue, but we walked in none-theless.

Tolya lay in an unpainted, rough pine coffin.

WE CARRIED the coffin into the bus. There were nine of us: three women, two boys, and four men. The bus pulled up to the church, and we carried the coffin inside. Our escort, too, walked into the church and took off their hats. They stood apart from us.

The priest started the service. He conducted it with inspiration, and the choir of old ladies sang emotionally and with extraordinary beauty. The priest poured a hand-ful of soil into the coffin, and we nailed the lid shut. The old ladies, singing, followed the coffin to the bus.

The bus, followed by the Gazik, crossed the town line, negotiating the deserted road to the cemetery. The deep grave had already been dug; on top of it were two steel rods to lay the coffin on. Our men and boys, slipping on frozen clumps of ground, carried the coffin to the grave. Pasha, too, carried his father's coffin.

It was windy, and there was no one out, just Tolya's guards and us. Everything was ready, the shovels, the long white towel. But they realized that we would not let them near the grave, so they stayed away "until the end of the operation," as one of them put it.

Tolya's friends said a few words of farewell over the grave. We started covering the grave, first with our hands, then with shovels. An hour later we had put together a high mound. On top of it we laid live and artificial flowers, apples, bread crumbs. We put up a white pine cross; I hope it was made by prisoners. With a ballpoint pen, I wrote on the cross: "Anatoly Marchenko. 23/1/1938–8/12/1986."*

ALL THOSE DAYS, December 10, 11, and 12, I did my best to ascertain the circumstances surrounding my husband's death. My efforts were unsuccessful.

It was impossible to break through the shroud of secrecy around the final months of Marchenko's life. There is a reason for that secrecy: they wanted to bury more than Anatoly's body; they wanted to bury the significance of his entire life, the significance of his struggle in those last months.

The authorities keep lying, evading answers, and simply avoiding me. The true diagnosis is being kept from me. Almeyev told me that death was caused by irreversible cardiopulmonary insufficiency resulting from cardiomyopathy. But the neurologist at the city hospital who saw Marchenko just before his death told us that he was brought in with interruptions of breathing, swallowing, and speech functions. According to that doctor, Anatoly died of a vertebrobasilar insufficiency, a stroke. Which of them is to believed? The prison doctor has reasons to

---

*Written in the European style. Marchenko was born on January 23, 1938, and died December 8, 1986. (Trans.)

insist on the heart disease story: the authorities fear that I will refer to the December 1983 incident when the guards at a Perm camp pounded Marchenko's head against the cement floor. They pounded him until he became unconscious, then dropped him on the punishment cell floor, his handcuffs still on. His breathing was disrupted, and it was only on demand from other prisoners who heard his wheezing that he received medical attention. For several days Anatoly felt acute results of the beating: irregularities of vision, sense of smell, and sense of taste. That incident didn't pass without a trace. Over the last three years he suffered from recurring headaches and dizzy spells. I am not a doctor, but it is clear even to me that the neurological consequences of the beating could have led to disruption of blood flow to the brain; that is, if you believe that version.

But even the other version of the cause of death cannot obscure the truth. After all, the "cardiopulmonary insufficiency resulting from cardiomyopathy" is nothing but the result of the hunger strike he had held since August 4.

In either case, Anatoly didn't die of "natural causes," as I was assured. It was the prison that killed him.

At the same time, I was not told about the circumstances of his illness. Two weeks before my husband's death, at the KGB, I was told that he was in "excellent health." On December 11, while he was answering my questions about the final weeks of Marchenko's life, Political Officer Churbanov's tongue slipped. "He got up every now and then," he said. That could mean just one thing: that Anatoly's condition was poor long before his death. A day earlier, on December 10, Almeyev said: "His health suddenly deteriorated and we immediately sent him to a hospital." As I recently found out, that same day, in Moscow, officials told Western reporters that "Marchenko died as a result of a prolonged, serious illness."

Lies and inconsistencies surround the circumstances of Anatoly Marchenko's life in prison.

"Why was my husband deprived of visits, placed in punishment cells, transferred from regular prison regimen to strict?" I asked Churbanov. (Strict prison regimen is the harshest in the country, and Marchenko had experienced it many a time.)

"Actually, we never had any complaints about Marchenko," Churbanov suddenly answered.

If not they, then who? Should this be taken to mean that they were acting in accordance with some high authority, which had decided that Marchenko was to perish? Or could it be that Churbanov was simply trying to evade blame for my husband's death? The political officer assured me that Marchenko was not forced to work in prison, that he "wasn't required to fill his work quota," yet, on another occasion, he read from an order of August 1986: "To deprive Marchenko of a visit for malicious nonfulfillment of the quota." He would say that no KGB official ever had contact with Marchenko, then his tongue would slip and he'd say, "How should I know? They have free access. They don't report to me."

But at the core of his lies was the lie about the hunger strike.

When I asked if my husband had been on a hunger strike, and, if so, when it began and when it ended, Churbanov didn't dare say no. Nor did he tell the truth. His exact words: "Sometimes he starved, sometimes no, it varied."

"What were the exact dates?"

"You know, I can't recall."

This was repeated several times.

Anyone who knew Tolya would see that the claims that he started several hunger strikes, then stopped them are nothing but a lie.

Here is what I know from several reliable sources, not all of whom can be named:

On August 4, 1986, Marchenko started a hunger strike. It's not clear whether it continued to his death or was called off late in November. We'll return to that later. But it is certain that in August, September, October, and part of November, Anatoly was on a hunger strike.

Immediately after calling the strike he was transferred to strict prison regimen. In another two days he was deprived of a visit with me and our son. What else was done with him I don't yet know, but Marchenko did not end his strike in August, September, or October.

Sometime after October 8 his strict regimen was prolonged, and soon something important happened, something I cannot yet account for: Marchenko was either taken out of Chistopol, or, for a month, he was kept in a solitary punishment cell. I have reasons to believe that the latter is more likely. That means that during the third month of the hunger strike he was deprived of warm clothes, a mattress, and a blanket; he was not receiving letters, books, or magazines, and was not allowed to write. Anatoly was being killed.

My question to Churbanov: "Was he force-fed?"

"No, no, why?"

That's a lie, I hope.

The prison's administration says that early in November, Marchenko was transferred to the prison's hospital ward, where he was receiving dietetic food. That's a lie. The hunger strike continued.

In November, international pressure to free Anatoly

Marchenko escalated. The authorities were considering the chances of starting to negotiate with me on that matter. Meanwhile, Marchenko starved, and his condition was approaching the critical point.

On November 13 the negotiations began. That day I talked to a high-level party official, who, as he put it, was authorized to respond to my letter to the general secretary of the CPSU. (It was January when I sent a letter, in which I asked Gorbachev to intervene on Marchenko's behalf, but the time for the "response" arrived only now, when the world was demanding Marchenko's release, and he was dying in Chistopol.) The party official suggested that I petition for my husband's pardon. I sent the petition out on November 20.

On November 21, the KGB suggested that Anatoly, our son, and I promptly emigrate to Israel. "We need your decision immediately," officials Topolev and Belov insisted, "on behalf of the superiors." I demanded a meeting with my husband. "There will be no meeting, but you may submit a written request for a meeting." I did.

I believe that two days later my husband ended the hunger strike. Two clues point to that: on November 26, in Chistopol, my husband suddenly received five rubles' worth of merchandise from the prison store. I learned about this through an entry in his prison account, which, by the mistake of prison officials, fell into my hands. It revealed a great deal. (Among other things, it confirmed that the hunger strike continued uninterrupted from August through November.)

But the entry, dated November 26, does not show Marchenko's signature. That means he did not request food. To them he made no requests. But they had orders: get Marchenko on his feet, make the withered man fit to be shown to me, or, in case we agreed to emigrate, to the West.

There was another clue: on November 28, Tolya sent me a letter with a request for a food parcel, to be sent to him in care of the prison's sick ward. At the time, he was not entitled either to write a letter or to receive a parcel. If that letter is genuine, either he had ended the hunger strike or, possibly, he was preparing to end it.

Whether or not Anatoly ended the hunger strike, it is beyond doubt that, in late November, his health took a sharp turn for the worse. Whether it was a stroke or something else, it is clear that now he was dying. Still, even at that time I was not allowed to see my husband. His death was anything but unexpected for prison officials, no matter how much they try to convince me otherwise.

Now, the main thing: the principal demand of the hunger strike was the release of political prisoners in the USSR. I know this for certain: Marchenko's hunger strike, which he began on August 4, was supposed to continue at least through May 4 of the next year. No relaxations of the regime, no concessions to Marchenko personally could end the strike. The only possible explanation for the end of the hunger strike (if it was indeed ended) is that my husband was told that the question of amnesty of political prisoners would be resolved in the near future. Who could have told him? Apparently one of the high-placed officials who came from Moscow to see him on November 25 and 26.

WHAT DID Marchenko die of?

The diagnoses given to me contradict each other. They were oral communications. Deceitful oral communications. Nobody gave me my husband's death certifi-

213

cate. The medical records were never shown to me. They refused to let me have as much as an abstract. Or even to read them to me. I was not given, or even allowed to read, the autopsy report. I didn't receive so much as a certificate of burial.

So I have no documents connected with my husband's death. Just the telegram. Of course, it's not a certified telegram, which means it, too, does not constitute a document.

I did not receive the letters Marchenko got from friends, the photographs that were in his possession, my last letters to him. I did not get any of the journals my husband kept. And I know for certain that he kept them. I did not receive his notes on clippings from newspapers and magazines.

I did not receive my husband's last letter to me, the letter that he was writing in October and was supposed to have mailed in the first days of December. Why? For just one reason: the authorities feared that these notes would reveal the circumstances of the last days in the life of Anatoly Marchenko.

The secrecy that surrounds my husband's demise fails to obscure the point: Anatoly Marchenko died in battle. For him, that battle had begun a quarter of a century earlier, and he had never—never—raised the white flag of truce. For twenty of those twenty-five years, his battle was waged in prison cells, camp barracks, internal exile. Anatoly could have lived free, but he deliberately chose prison. He chose prison so others would live in freedom.

I am boundlessly grateful to those who took part in my husband's fate. I beseech you, those of you who are near, and those of you who are far, do not forget that the "Marchenko case" is not closed. The complete amnesty of all political prisoners, freedom to all political prisoners—that is the sacred cause for which Anatoly laid down his life, that is the cause for which he starved for the last four months of his life, that is the cause for which he died in the horrible Chistopol Prison on December 8, 1986.

Moscow
December 13–14, 1986

A CHRONOLOGY
OF THE LIFE OF
ANATOLY MARCHENKO

1938   Born January 23 in a worker's family in the town of Barabinsk along the trans-Siberian railroad.

1958   Sentenced to two years' imprisonment for taking part in a fight in his workers' dormitory. Actually, he was trying to break up the fight. Escapes from prison after a year; goes into hiding.

1960   Attempts unsuccessfully to cross the border to Iran (October 29).

1961   Convicted of treason and sentenced to six years in the camps (March 3). In the camps he meets Moscow intellectuals, including the writer, Yuli Daniel, convicted for publishing in the West.

1966   Finds himself among the politically active Moscow *intelligentsia*.

1967   Completes *My Testimony*, a witness account of post-Stalin ¹ bor camps.

1968   Sentenced August 21 to one year in the camps for living in Moscow without a residency permit.*

---

*Marchenko was arrested on July 29, 1968, a week after sending an open letter to the Czechoslovak *Rude Pravo* and *Literarny Listy*, as

In prison, hears that seven of his Moscow friends, including Daniel's former wife, Larisa Bogoraz, went out on Red Square on August 25 to protest the invasion of Czechoslovakia.

1969   Rearrested in the camp and sentenced to two years under trumped-up charges of slandering the Soviet system to inmates and guards. Sentenced August 26 to two years in the camps.

My Testimony published in Russian in the West and translated into every major language.

1971   Released from the camp July 29.

1973   Marries Bogoraz. The couple have a son, Pavel.

1975   Sentenced March 31 to four years in internal exile under the manufactured charges of living in Moscow without a residency permit.

---

well as the BBC, Izvestia, Pratze, L'Humanité, L'Unita, and The Morning Star. In the letter, Marchenko expressed his "respect for and sympathy toward the process of democratization in Czechoslovakia" and said he feared that the Soviets would resort to an invasion to put an end to Prague Spring: "Are our leaders indeed distressed by the events in Czechoslovakia? I think they are more than distressed. They are frightened. It is not because these changes represent a threat to socialism or to security of the Warsaw Pact countries. They are frightened because these changes have the potential to undermine the authority of leadership in those countries and discredit the methodology of governance which currently prevails in the socialist camp."

Marchenko and his friends were convinced that the letter was the direct cause of his arrest. (Trans.)

Writes *From Tarusa to Chuna,* which appears in the West in 1977.

1979   Released from internal exile and given an ultimatum to emigrate or go to prison. Ignores the ultimatum.

1981   Sentenced September 4 to ten years in strict-regimen camp and five in internal exile. The accusations include the writing of this book.

1983   Severely beaten on the head by guards and, as a consequence, suffers from dizzy spells and blackouts (December).

1986   Goes on a hunger strike, demanding release of all political prisoners and criminal prosecution of the jailers who had beaten him.

Dies in Chistopol Prison December 8.

INDEX

Escape from USSR, decision concerning, 2–3, 5

Father. *See* Marchenko (father)
Flaubert, 159
Friends
  anonymity of, in writings, 129
  birthday party given by, 15–16
  concern about Marchenko's fate, 90–91
  defense attorney provided by, 193–94
  at first trial, 122–23
  Red Square demonstration by, after Prague invasion, 128–29
  support from, 14–15, 118
Funeral, Marchenko's, 207–8
Fedya. *See* Fyodor
Fyodor (uncle), 46–49

Gambling
  in prison camps, 146–47
  in Solikamsk prison, 135–37
Ginzburg, Aleksandr, 10, 16, 116
Ginzburga, Ludmilla Ilynichna (mother of Ginzburg), 116–17
Gnevkovskaya (investigator), 12
Godmother. *See* Lyolka
Gorbachev, Mikhail, 212
Gorky, Maxim, 164–65
Grigory (childhood friend), 37–38

Heart of a Dog, The (Mikhail Bulgakov), 15
Homosexuals, 163
Hunger strike, 210–13

Illness(es), 14–15, 50
Intelligentsia (intellectuals)
  attitude toward, in provinces, 6–7

bravery of, 118
differentiated from professionals, 7–8
government officials' attitudes toward, 12
living conditions of, 3–4, 8–9, 11–12
Interrogations
  fellow prisoners at, 185–87
  by Kamayev and Antonov, 177–79

Jokes, 36, 64–65, 183, 188–89

Kamayev (procurator), 171
  announcement of charges under Article 190-1 by, 163–65
  incorrect identification of Marchenko in lineup by Rybalko and, 181–85
  and KGB chief officer Antonov, interrogation by, 177–79
  presentation of depositions by, 167–69
Kaminskaya, Dina Isaakovna, 122–23, 187, 190
  replaced, 193–94
KGB. *See also* Antonov; Medvedev
  chase in metro station, 106–7
  escape from agents of, 93–96
  Galina Borisovna, pseudonym for, 84–85
  meeting with N.P. during, 102–4
  My Testimony and, 85, 119
  prisoners' testimony used by, 167
  questioning by, in Nyrob prison camp, 158–59
  questioning by Medvedev (KGB agent), 108–12